Rugby Stories
from the Platteland

Graham Jooste

Published in 2005 by 30° South Publishers (Pty) Ltd.
28, 9th Street, Newlands, 2092
Johannesburg, South Africa
www.30degreessouth.co.za

Copyright © Graham Jooste, 2005

Cover artwork and cartoons by Brian Schwarz, East London
Design and origination by Kerrin Cocks
Printed and bound by Pinetown Printers (Pty) Ltd.

ISBN 0-9584890-1-7

By the same author:

Innocent Blood (2002)
So Het Hulle Gesterf (1998)
Rugby Trivia (1995)
South African Rugby Teams: 1949–1995 (1995)

CONTENTS

INTRODUCTION

THIS BOOK IS DEDICATED to all those brave men and boys who dared to play the national game of rugby on the platteland so many years ago.

My unending, reverential wonder and awe inspired me to attempt to put pen to paper to try and capture something of this bygone era before it is too late. The pride and joy of wearing the jersey and socks of the dorp's rugby team, the selection squabbles, the dusty fields, the women committees, the transport arrangements and the struggle to find referees, were all part of a strong foundation laid for future generations of stars to build upon.

Whenever somebody new arrived in these small South African towns he was immediately approached to find out whether he had played the game before, be he a new bank clerk, post office assistant, policeman, railway worker, magistrate's clerk, schoolteacher, Public Works Department employee, stock and dipping inspector, co-operative worker, mechanic, wool agent, hides and skins buyer or relief barman.

The thought behind this instant approach was to find out whether the newly arrived individual would be able to assist the local side if called upon to do battle with a neighbouring dorpspan. The newcomer felt flattered by the attention, the community had done its duty in extending such an invitation and with luck, might have stumbled upon a gem. Thus the newly arrived person was accepted into the community of rugby.

The larger towns in the various provinces supplied

the majority of players in the Currie Cup Tournament as it was then called. The provinces were Border, Eastern Province, Griqualand West, Northern Transvaal, Orange Free State, Transvaal, Western Province, North Eastern Districts and Natal. At a later stage more unions were formed, the likes of Western Transvaal, Eastern Transvaal and Rhodesia. With the expansion of the game over a period of time such teams as Northern Free State, Far North, Northern Natal, Boland, South Western Districts, North West Cape and South Eastern Transvaal emerged from platteland slumber to enter the arena of the groot manne competition ... not to mention South West Africa, Stellaland and Lowveld. The likes of Vaal Triangle and Eastern Free State chipped in as well.

Leading up to this explosion of the smaller unions into the 'big time', the aim of every serious player in these smaller areas was to make it into the sub-union side of a leading province. For example, there was the Free State (South) sub-union, which encompassed the towns of Zastron, Rouxville, Smithfield and Wepener among others. Other larger unions also had their demarcated districts for the sub-union system. Eastern Free State actually became a fully fledged union and had a go at the larger unions. The sub-unions competed with each other and it was at these games that the platteland hopefuls might catch the eyes of the union selectors.

We must also remember that a pool of players was created by geographical situations. For instance, the old Transkei was a prime example of a district that supplied players to the local town sides. Sons of traders and farmers were sent to one of the three great rugby schools situated in East London, Kingwilliamstown and Queenstown. Also, we must not forget the Grahamstown connection and Rhodes University. During the school holidays these students were often drafted into teams like Pirates of Umtata, Butterworth, Idutywa, Engcobo, Ugie, Maclear and Elliot. The situation was similar in other parts of South Africa as well. This was an accepted feature as long as dad paid his son's subscription and the boy attended at least one practice ... in order to qualify!

The same applied to police-college trainees and boys from the armed forces, home on leave, helping serve behind the counter at the family trading store or farm store. Spectators were always interested in seeing how a son of the community had progressed while away from home. The occasion was also one for socializing and renewing friendships. The annual rugby dance was an occasion not to be missed. Many made a supreme effort to attend these functions although far from the dorpie. Socially, this event played a huge role in the far-flung communities and on occasions became somewhat hectic, to say the least! The standard rule was that all festivities had to cease at midnight, as the following day was a Sunday.

Sadly, all these traditions and customs have been whittled away by various factors and are no more. Those of us who were fortunate enough to have been part of this institution will always look back and be thankful for the oppurtunity of being a part of it.

I cannot apologize for any grammatical errors. These stories have been put to paper as I heard them. Many of them were told to me by men from the platteland who were not well versed in English and many was the time that they tried to impress the listeners with their knowledge of English. Many of them would switch from Afrikaans into English and vice versa when stuck for a word or two. I sincerely hope that you the reader will accordingly accept this and realize that some of these tales were told by people whose passion for the game surpassed their educational qualifications.

On the platteland, the local dorp rugby headquarters was always the local hotel. There always seemed to be a Royal Hotel, Commercial Hotel or Grand Hotel! After practices on dusty fields everybody would congregate at these venues to slake his thirst and have a bath or shower in the facilities at the end of a long, dark passage lit only by a dim lightbulb. The presidents and coaches of these teams were usually elderly men and appeared to be dignified by the positions 'thrust' upon them at the Annual General Meeting, which had preceeded the playing season. They were proud of the responsibilities handed to them and often shared the same status as the burgermeesters of the various dorpe.

The local ladies were always involved by providing eats and beverages of a non-alchoholic nature at the matches and quietly glowed with pride when a family member showed prowess on the field. The profits from these stalls went to the club and were usually used to compensate those club members who had cars and carted the team around. Jerseys and socks were to be had at the local store or farmers' co-operative. The players had to buy these themselves. Numbers on the

11

jerseys were not included. It was a familiar sight to see a farmer coming to town for provisions, wearing his team jersey or socks with his veldskoene ... and many of the townsmen used the jersey for their gardening attire! The jersey was worn with pride—a sort of status symbol. This simplicity has now disappeared forever.

I hope I can capture for you the passion and atmosphere of a grand old era in the following pages.

Some names may have been changed to protect the offenders and the guilty.

Graham Jooste
Johannesburg, 2005

AN IRISH CONNECTION

Safe upon the shores of England and still following the game, I met an elderly Irishman who told me this story at his favourite watering hole in Liverpool.

ON THE ISLE OF Inishmaan, there was no sport! We only had currachs and loading pigs for the market at Galway across the bay. My grandfather was evicted from his stone cottage by the commissioner because of rent, you follow. He came across the sea to here and got a job on a collier plying out of Swansea. He once went to see a strange game played by men with an egg-shaped ball that bounced all over the place.

It was a Saturday afternoon and his collier, the *Brechin*, was high and dry having repairs and her bottom scraped. As he looked after the ropes, and the ropes were not needed that day because she was out of the water he went with some of his friends to this game.

He had some money from the union man but hitched a lift from some Godfearing soul all the way to the St. Helen's ground, named after St. Helen, you know. He was in time and saw fifteen men in dark-green jerseys with a springbok on the pocket. They were running onto the field and the people were clapping and shouting instructions to them.

Another group ran onto the field in red jerseys and the shouting got louder and louder! This was the side from Wales, you follow. My grandfather explained to me that the men in green were from the tip of Africa and had sailed all the way to play this game over here. Now the men from Africa had names like Uncle, Klondyck, Bingo and Mary* by gorrah, could you believe that an' all!

The men charged at each other, got down on the knees and pushed, fighting over this ball. Somebody got a black eye and was treated with water poured over his head. The men in green were very big and called to each other in a foreign language. When they fell on the ball behind the posts, they all had to start again from the middle of the field. After the game he met some trawlermen who could not remember who won the game but thought it was the foreigners. They thought so because we saw them doing a pagan dance behind the sitting stand long after the game!

He thought to himself that if a person could run with a ball under his arm and have so many people shouting at him he should ask Father O' Callaghan about it all. After many days of thinking about this game he told me that I should try to play it one day.

After selling all my newspapers at Charing Cross that day I went to see a game for myself. I was very excited when I got into the ground because a side was called the London Irish and they were strangers to me! Nobody spoke Gaelic and most cursed in English as well. When a side scored everybody threw their hats in the air. I did the same and some urchin ran off with it. I did not chase him because I got a better one and sat on it to hide it away, you know.

After the game I asked the landlord of the side if I could play this game for him. He told me to join the

London Scottish, I ask you! That is my story.

More pints and talking to him revealed that he knew of a side called Guys Hospital. He explained in great detail that the young doctors played this game purely for financial gain and that he had permission to sell his newspapers to their victims while they were recovering in hospital. His old grandfather was indeed correct: "Follow this pagan festival and you will be delighted, my boy."

*F. 'Uncle' Dobbin—scrumhalf (Griqualand West)
J. 'Klondyck' Raaff—wing forward (Griqualand West)
K.W. 'Bingo' Burger—frontranker (Border)
D. 'Mary' Jackson—frontranker (Western Province)

THE FREE STATE TRIANGLE

THERE WAS THIS HOTEL you see! It was in Smithfield and it was called the Royal Hotel. I will never know why it was called Royal because this has always been Hertzog territory since the Boer War days. Anyway, I am sure the English had something to do with it because they liked to exploit us. They might have known that the nearest place you could get really good mampoer was near Rustenburg and that the transport riders were mostly occupied in carting dynamite for the Transvaal mines. My grandfather told me that this was the reason why an Englishman opened the first hotel here. To make a profit out of them all!

The Smithfield Hotel.

The market place opposite the hotel.

But us Boers had a good idea what was going on, so we formed a pact among ourselves. This pact told us that if anyone of us had to have a drink in this hotel, it would only be one, then 'opsaal' and home. It also gave the owner the message that we were merely tolerating him and checking up on him from time to time, you understand, hey? So good!

Man this treaty among the Boers went on for a very long time until a rugby player forced a kind of an amendment to the Act, so to say. They say it happened just after Boetie McHardy became the first Free Stater to play for the Springboks in 1912 and scored a try against Scotland where the Bokke won 16-0 in Edinburgh. After every try he scored on that tour they would have a drink for him at the hotel to upset the owner, you see!

Man, it later became blêrrie complicated because they were drinking to the health of Boetie, with English beer, and they had to pay for it. The older men tried to talk some sense into the heads of the younger men who were now playing rugby and liked to have a beer after the game.

My father then told me that things were getting a bit tense in the district because some players were having an extra doppie for the Union as well! You know man, the new Union of South Africa, which started in 1910. Okay?

Anyway, as I was saying. Oh, yes, I think the whole business blew up at the birth of Kerneel's boytjie. You see, what happened was that after a practice game one Wednesday they all went to the hotel for only one drink. Kerneels thought it was a good idea to wet the head of his young Casper, who was named after his oupa, called Kassie.

He ordered that extra dop for all the manne who were at the practice but also included everybody in the bar. In the bar were two English soldiers going home to England who were catching the ship in East London. It looked like they were chommies of the hotel owner, who was also a rooinek like them.

Man, I tell you it must have been damn complicated.

Now a person's pride comes into the picture, you see.

Kerneels raised his glass and bellowed, "Geluk manne!"

All the players shouted back, "Geluk, ook so!"

Three men answered with, "Cheers!"

A kind of stillness came over the bar. Kerneels was now in a hell of a spot. He had just bought two Tommies and an Englishman a drink and had raised glasses with them. But so had everybody else!

The English were making a profit out of him and he was also paying for them. Nobody knew what to say and some were looking at the ceiling.

But Kerneels was a clever frontranker and shouted out loud, "Here is to young Casper, who will play for Smithfield, Orange Free State and the Springboks and beat the hell out of the English!"

Everybody raised their glasses and shouted, "Hoor, hoor!" and stamped their feet on the plank floor.

The Tommies raised their glasses and answered, "Hear, hear! Here is to you all! Cheers, and all that, and to your son!"

The owner gave everybody another beer, on the house. Some of the men eyed the bottles put in front of them from a distance while a few stared at the ceiling above them. Poor old Sakkie did not know what to do. He lifted his bottle, then put it down and wiped his hand on his dusty practice jersey.

What was going on here? Boers buying drinks for the Tommies and the Tommies buying drinks for the Boere. Everybody started talking about Boetie's three tries against the Irish and bets were being taken how many he would score against the English. Tom

Clarke, the owner, now started writing it all down in an old exercise book and everybody paid in a sixpence. Somebody groaned that the dominee must never hear about this or else there would be groot kak in die land! Gambling was a serious sin. Vlekkie muttered something about how Sannie would never wash his rugby jersey again because it was stained with English beer.

The day was saved by old Willie, the local scab inspector. He explained a story about never to look a horse that has been given to you in the mouth, or something like that, ou maat. He went on to tell them that the drinks were a gift to them all and also to Boytjie Casper, who will one day play for Smithfield, Orange Free State and the Springboks against the English. He also told them that the Tommies thought that they were the best side in the southern Free State and would tell the people in England about them. Kosie mentioned that he now understood what was going on and that the scab inspector had such good logic that he should stand for the Volksraad next year. One by one the men nodded to the Tommies and drifted out, satisfied about their pride and the future of rugby in Smithfield.

Anyway, as the years went by, and the rebellion was over and done with, a gentle sort of peace settled over the district. By now the dorpies of Zastron and Rouxville were also getting sides together. The three towns started playing against each other and it was becoming a great outing for the people on Saturday afternoons. These games were always played at the municipal showgrounds but the rugby club had to pay for the posts, you know. During the winter months the little grass that there was on the surface turned into a choking dust.

Ja, now, in any case, listen to this story, ou maat. Yes, thanks, I will have another doppie.

As I was saying, the biggest supporter Smithfield had was Oom Jacob. He once played for us at scrumhalf because half the team was down with the griep but they were determined to put a side together to play Rouxville. Smithfield would never cancel a game and give away points. He was the town engineer who was in charge of the night pans, you know. He had two carts, five horses, two drivers, four runners and about fifty pans under his control, not counting the school and hotel.

The old stand at the Rouxville showgrounds.

By now, ou Tom was allowing us to use a room in his hotel to change in and a separate one for visiting teams. The two bedrooms nearest the bar were used for that purpose. The players thought that this was a luxury because somebody had stolen the wooden seats at the showgrounds where they used to change and it was difficult to change standing up. If they sat down their pants would be covered in dust before they ran onto the field. You know how it is, mos, those blêrrie people could have taken bluegum branches instead!

PAWILJOEN OPGERIG MET
HULP VAN DEPARTEMENT VAN
ONDERWYS KUNS & WETENSKAP

The changeroom under the stand.

The rows of bluegums at the old showgrounds.

What colour was our jerseys? Okay, I will tell you. Smithfield was green, Rouxville was blue and Zastron was maroon, all with white pants. Man, I tell you a game between these sides, was a game! Anyway, you know, there was once a helse family fight because of rugby. It was like this, I will not tell you the names because some people are still cross about it. This outjie was a member of the Smithfield co-op who farmed in the Rouxville district but played rugby for Zastron! Everybody screamed "Treason!" or something like that! He was a helse good flyhalf and all three sides claimed him.

He was also stubborn and his father's threats about inheritance and farms belonging to the family did not worry him because he was visiting a farmer's daughter in the Zastron district. This big family split into three separate bodies and argued until all the Afrikaner cattle came home. You know what I mean, hey! You see that small market place across from the hotel there? That is where a helse argument broke loose on market day. One cousin got so bedondered that he took his banking account to Aliwal North to be out of it! Ja, I'm not bluffing, ou maat. It got so hotted up that the dominee from Rouxville had to interfere and ask for help from the dominees of the other two towns.

His own mother told the whole family that they were dom and stupid and that she was very fond of his nooientjie and that he should play for Zastron because she was from there. Her husband, his father, told her that this was business for the men to decide and she told him to go and sleep in the spare room on the stoep.

In elk geval, the day happened when Zastron came

to play Smithfield. Oom Jacob who by now was so gatvol over the whole affair that he decided to tell everybody what he thought when the bar opened that Saturday morning before the game. He walked in just as Tom unlocked the door over there and pushed the batwing doors open to see if the stoep had been swept after the dust storm.

Oom Jacob ordered his first Commando brandy and water. He opened a new packet of Commando Cork 50s, tapped the end violently on the lid, lit up with his matches and replaced the used one back into the box. He was ready for action as he blew out a huge puff of smoke. He shuffled around on his favourite barstool there near the door and had his first sluk. The first of many on that memorable day. Jannie, the young barman for the day, arrived and ou Tom dissappeared to the safety of his front office.

Oom Jacob decided that as there was nobody to listen to him except for Jannie he would tell him a thing or two about this three-cornered affair. He started by telling Jannie that he only drank Commando brandy for a blêrrie good reason. The reason was that if Jannie looked carefully at the label on the bottle he would see a commando led by the general from this district. That went to prove that it was the best brandy in South Africa. He then went on to say that everybody around here should be like him and drink Commando and smoke Commando out of loyalty.

"Loyalty! Talking about loyalty! No such blêrrie thing exists anymore!" he snorted.

Take for example the flyhalf playing for Zastron, who is a member of Smithfield co-op.

26

"A big shame, that's what it is," he said. "Everybody was buggering off to wherever they wanted to. If everybody did this what will happen to my job?" He was getting worried because he only had a few years to go for his pension. Oh, yes, he had also heard that there was a new kind of toilet being used on the Reef! If this came to Smithfield, he would be staring disaster in the face. Have the dorpsraad considered that! He would tell them a thing or two my swaertjie when the time comes around.

What would happen to his night-soil horses, old Roberts, Kitchener, Milner, Rhodes and Chamberlain?

"What about the three pounds, two and sixpence that my senior driver Stompie had borrowed from me five years ago for lobola? No, no, sorry, he paid me two shillings off last year. You see these hands, my boet? A workingman's hands that have mended reins and saddles and stitched bridles. Hard work! For what? Everything is changing so fast. No more loyalty! Things are not right in the land.

"You take for example this same Stompie of mine. He tells me that Hennie should play on the wing because he runs like a vlakhaas because he is scared with the ball in his hands. That was a helse thing to say to me, his baas. I told him that I would tell Hennie what he had said if he did not to start paying me back his debt. Stompie went nearly white because he knows that mechanic's temper, my boet. I did not tell Hennie because then I would have lost a driver. Teach him right, that's me, my boet. I'm the wrong oke to sukkel with. Ja, give me a double!"

Now Jannie the barman noticed that Oom Jacob

27

was missing the counter with his elbow every now and then. Maybe it was because he moved his stool a bit further back after his last visit to the kleinhuisie outside. After his return he had another complaint, you see. He reported that there was only one match left in the box there, and what would have happened if he could not have lighted the candle stuck onto the Sunlight Polish tin lid.

It was blêrrie dark in there when the door was closed and you could hardly find a piece of *The Friend* newspaper stuck onto that six-inch nail. He told Jannie that his father had told him that Lord Roberts had started it. No, no, man, not the six-inch nail, but *The Friend* newspaper in Bloemfontein during the Boer War! Jannie poured Oom Jacob another Commando and settled down with his collection of 'Jakkals en Wolf' cartoons pasted into his scrapbook.

The silence was broken by hooters being blowed outside as the Zastron boys trooped into the bar on their way to Room 12. Smithfield always used Room 13, as it was closer to the bathroom. In a few minutes a couple of Zastron players were loosening up by running on the spot in the passage. The rest of the team joined them and they were busy singing:

> *O, moenie huil nie!*
> *O, moenie treur nie!*
> *Want die Zastron boys kom weer!*

when some Smithfield players arrived. Handshakes all round as friends greeted each other.

The Smithfield coach, Buks, assured his players

that a team that sings before a game cries after a game during his pep talk. This seemed to settle some players down as they trudged through the bar to their cars, smelling of Wintergreen. They assembled on the stoep and watched as a few Zastron windgatte decided to show their fitness by jogging to the showgrounds field there by the bluegums. They were followed by twenty young boys from the location.

The convoy of cars and groups of supporters all departed leaving Oom Jacob wondering how things had happened so suddenly around him. Jannie the barman was all brom-brom because he had to stay open in case of passing traffic and would not be able to watch the game. Anyway he still had Oom Jacob as company, who had decided to boycott the whole nasty affair. Everything was so quiet all of a sudden. Oom Jacob thudded another Commando Cork on the lid and had a good sluk. Jannie started reading a Mickey Mouse comic.

About fifteen minutes later the car hooters started blowing and Jannie ran to the door. He came back complaining that all he could see was dust, trees and cars parked in the sun. Oom Jacob assured him that Smithfield had scored because it sounded like Grootjan's new Ford truck. Grootjan would never blow his hooter for Zastron. Mind you, he did have relatives in that area, so you never knew … no, not Grootjan! Yes, it was a score for Smithfield … he just felt it in his water.

Again the hooters blew and Jannie and Oom Jacob looked at each other in silence as Oom pushed his glass forward for a refill. Later, somebody blew a little tune on his hooter! Oom muttered that Zastron had scored because he knew of nobody from here who would blow his hooter like that. Maybe it was a good tackle or something like that.

Anyway, it was about this time that Swartbaard Swart walked in feeling very bedônerd because he had got a puncture coming in from Swartlaagte to see the game. He nodded greetings and Oom Jacob nodded back very slowly with a faraway look in his eyes. Swartbaard downed a quick brandy and somebody from outside shouted that Zastron were leading by two points with very little time left. Oom Jacob bolted upright as a long blast of hooters followed. They just kept on blowing and Swartbaard rushed back in again.

With complete content Oom Jacob sighed and fell into a peace-like trance of self-satisfaction. He knew the result. He had fought a long and hard battle and took no notice what Swartbaard was saying. Occasionally he squared his shoulders, stuck his chin out and gazed at his half-empty glass. People swore that he was fast asleep in a sitting position. A slight grin never left his face, man, I tell you!

By now the bar was filling up with players and spectators in dribs and drabs as the Englishmen says. Some were limping, Kobie had a dirty bandage around his head and some were laughing. You should have seen ou Bakkies, you see! All you could see was two white eyes; the rest was dust and sweat all mixed up on his face. There was even dust sticking to the inside of his ears, I tell you!

Now everybody could not have a bath at the same time, so some of the blokes stayed in the bar while some went to clean up. After a while or so you heard singing from the bathroom:

> *O, moenie huil nie!*
> *O, moenie treur nie!*
> *Want die Smithfield boys is hier!*

It got louder and louder and some in the bar joined in as well. The bar started to fill up now and Jannie the barman had to know his story, I tell you. The owner, Tom, also had to come through and help a hand you know. The players who did not change first had no money on them so Jannie and Tom Clarke kept a record in that old school exercise book you see there. Well, ou maat, the party got off to a flying start as they say, when Tom bought a round all around. He was really not such a bad rooinek, you know!

Our president, ou Kobus got into the mood and also decided to buy a round and take it off from Hymie's account where all the Smithfield players had to buy their jerseys and socks. When more singing started Oom Jacob looked around like a rooster uplifting his head and became the conductor of great importance. He was a bit unsteady on his feet, gave a couple of sidesteps and bellowed out his contribution to the voices!

What happened next was talked about for the years to come. It happened like this. By now Oom Jacob had found his way back to that seat of his on the corner of the bar there close to the door leading onto the stoep. You see, meanwhile, Magasyn, the Smithfield flyhalf who had kicked the winning points, had fetched his

31

horse from his grandmother's stable here around the corner in that street close to the English church.

Some people heard the clip-clop on the stoep as Magasyn drove him gently through the batwing doors and into the bar! It came to stop at Oom Jacob's ear on the corner there. Oom Jacob did not see it because he was in a trance again. Oom Jacob must have felt the air from the nostrils of Mooinooi because he looked up right into the twitching nose of the horse.

He kind of let out a loud sigh and passed out on his barstool! He was blêrrie lucky because Flip, the Zastron lock, was passing by and caught him as he was sinking to the floor. He carried him gently and laid him on the bed in the Zastron bedroom. Some players followed and cleared the bed of togs and suitcases so that he could be comfortable, you see!

Well, the bar had to close at eleven o'clock because that was the law and we did not want to get Rassie the policeman into trouble. We all took our last-round drinks through to the front lounge.

One by one the blokes said goodbye to go home. Magasyn also wanted to get Mooinooi back to the stable. Silence settled over this small Free State dorpie again, but the snoring from Room 13 was something to hear!

About a week later Oom Jacob plucked up enough courage to go back to the bar to quietly ask if anybody had seen a horse in the bar the night Smithfield beat Zastron 9–8! They all expressed surprise at the constant question and kept the poor oubaas on a string for weeks thereafter. Much later Hettie from the telephone exchange put ou Jacob out of his misery and told him the truth.

He was so relieved that he went and bought Jannie a drink.

EVERYTHING HAPPENED AT THE Royal Hotel in Kuruman. It was the headquarters of the rugby club and they were having an emergency meeting after work in the bar. The future of the club was at stake because the tar road had now been completed and the men from the Provincial Roads Department were sure to be moved away somewhere else for another job.

Kallie Koekoemoer had captained the team for the last four years with good success against teams from Hotazel, Danielskuil, Olifantshoek and Vryburg. He played hooker because he liked people to support him. Nee, I'm just joking, you see! He was strong like an ox and also very clever and once played in the same team as Springbok Bennie Osler's cousin. That was in Somerset East in his younger days with the Cape Provincial Roads Department.

Kallie was the type of man that would give one hundred per cent and more if he believed what he was doing was the right thing, you know. You understand! Like the time when he had just put up his new 30 m.p.h. sign just outside of Wesselsvlei. A week later he was checking up on the road when he saw bullet holes right through the middel of the 0. He was so mad that his wife would not let him go to the Royal for a week, because he promised ugly things to the oke if he caught him.

Now it was summer and there were no rugby games or meetings anymore. Anyway, he started to do a bit of detective work on the quiet and decided to join the Kuruman Skietkommando. The kommandant was so impressed with his civil awareness that he borrowed him a Lee Metford and gave him fifty bullets as well.

Kallie went to all the shoots outside of the town and also brought his share of koeksisters and melktert that Sannie had made. During this time he noticed that a certain Fanus Combrink from a farm near to Wesselsvlei was a dekselse good shot with his Mauser. Anyway, one Saturday after the shoot all the manne went down to the Royal to get rid of the dust in their throats and talk about the coming Bisley in Upington next year.

During the talking later on in the evening Kallie mentioned that he had never seen such good grouping on a road sign he had seen somewhere. He could not remember where it was, he said. Fanus fell for the trap and said it was somewhere near Wesselsvlei.

On Monday, ou Kallie made out a document for ten gallons of petrol for the department lorry and drove out to Wesselsvlei. The sign was about a mile from the school and the church. Kallie stopped and had a good look at the damage to his new sign. His beautiful, shiny sign was neatly drilled in the middle of the 0 with rough edges sticking out at the back! Hell man, thought Kallie, this man can really shoot. Fanus had recently won the cup donated by the Boerekorporasie for the best shot of the year at the fundraising dance the month before.

Anyway, it was now time to talk to the suspect and save the taxpayer any future expenses because of this type of behaviour!

The farm road with the high middelmannetjie finally came out at a big farmhouse with a lot of chickens running around. Two lazy dogs barked a welcome and came sniffing at his boots. Fanus and his wife waved a friendly welcome and came to greet him.

Fanus, I think, was thinking that the P.W.D. were coming to inspect his road with the idea of putting a grader onto it. They went inside and had some coffee and rusks and spoke about farming and things like that. Kallie then asked Fanus to come with him along the road, as he wanted to discuss a matter with him. Fanus was all ears and the men went walking along the road with the dogs following.

Kallie started telling Fanus about the damaged road sign and that he could not understand why certain farmers shot holes through the department's signs and not their own platenames at the gates. Sometimes the farmers even got free ones from tractor companies and things like that! In any case the Chief of Provincial Administration in Cape Town was considering applying to the Chief Minister of Justice for the whole Cape Province to issue warrants of arrest for guilty parties. Those people would be arrested and transported to the Castle in Cape Town to await trial. Sometimes it would take up to three months for the suspect to appear in court!

Fanus was now listening very closely and swallowed hard. Did Fanus know anything about those nine bullet holes in the sign? No, he blurted out there was only three or so of his. The others were there long before his! Fanus was doomed and sat down on the big stone near the drift. He muttered something about his family and his crops. He fumbled for a Springbok cigarette, which Kallie lighted for him with his matches.

Fanus was now desperate and asked when all this

was going to take place. When would he have time to complete his ploughing for fodder for his cattle? Was there nothing that could be done, whispered Fanus to Kallie. Could Kallie not tell them that it was a joke and that there was no intention to damage government property? Could he not pay an admission of guilt so that he would not have to go down to Cape Town and face the court alone? He had never been in one before, and would not know what to do. Furthermore, his nearest relatives were in Pofadder and that's a hell of a long way from the Cape.

Kallie kept very quiet and kept looking at the sky. He puffed his pipe and suggested that there might just be a way around this dreadful business. Fanus promised anything so long as his family, the dominee and his bank manager never got to hear about this affair. He was ready to listen.

Fanus listened as Kallie explained in great detail that over the last three seasons the rugby club jerseys had been torn and mended over and over again by wives and mothers. With all the stitching and scrubbing it was now an embarassment to run onto the field in those blue and white colours. Everybody in the district should be proud of the team. Look how spic and span the Vryburg boys look when they run onto the field! All those good old values would be lost if nothing was ever done. The men would lose their self-respect and start to play shabby rugby! They would lose all their games and the name of Kuruman would mean nothing to anybody anymore.

Who would come to do business in the town if this area was not developed and encouraged to do better?

What would people do on a Saturday afternoon in winter if there was no rugby to follow? The youth of Kuruman would stay indoors and would not be healthy anymore. What would the doctors say? Hey, man, do you know that the hospital has only one sister and a nurse!

By this time poor Fanus was close to a breakdown as he lit his third Springbok in a row. Finally Kallie put his proposition to him, which Fanus accepted just like that! When the two men arrived back at the house Lettie asked her husband if he had seen a ghost because he was so pale. He laughed out aloud and said they had been inspecting the road.

About six weeks later a parcel arrived for the rugby club addressed to the Royal Hotel. It was opened at the next monthly meeting and inside was twenty brand-new jerseys with matching socks, I tell you, my boet! Now that was the first time in the history of the dorpspan that they had a complete set of new jerseys, all together, at one time. Normally the men had to buy them in Kimberley.

The parcel came from a sports shop in Johannesburg who would not answer the letter from the secretary as to who ordered the jerseys, but told them it was for the Kuruman Rugby Club and had been paid for in full. This now split the rugby club into two sections, who did some searching for souls, as the Englishman says.

The one group said that you should not look a horse that was a gift in the mouth. The other side said that the jerseys should be given to the postmaster for safekeeping and that after a year if nobody claimed them they could be bought by the players at a special knockdown price. The funds would go to the club. The dominee, as well as a missionary outside the town, was asked for his thoughts on the matter.

This parcel had now become the talking point of the entire district and Fanus was having nightmares, which baffled Lettie so much that she told Fanus to go to the new doctor in Vryburg for a complete check-up. Then the unbelievable happened. A telegram arrived on a dusty Friday and the delivery boy put it in his pouch and rushed over to the hotel with it.

It was signed for by Maxie Cohen the owner and also the president of the club. He opened it with shaking hands. Could this be a telegram from the police about that bottle of brandy he had raffled for club funds without asking the winner a question so as to comply with the Liquor Act?

He read it over and over again and dashed into the bar where eight members were sitting after work at the counter. He read the telegram to them. It was in English and said:

The donor of the parcel containing rugby jerseys and socks advises the Kuruman Rugby Club that the sender who will remain unknown bequethed the same in his will for your use. The matter is now considered closed and final!

Some of the boys let out a still whistle in wonder, you know! The word went around quickly about this strange telegram from lawyers as more and more members arrived to discuss this matter. The meeting took about five hours because now everybody was racking his brains as to who had died recently. Many glasses were raised and a festive mood prevailed. The party got bigger and bigger. One farmer said that he had heard of a thing the Irish do in Ireland when somebody dies it is called 'awake'. People were impressed and the new toast became 'Wakker!'.

Only two men knew the real secret, which was kept for twenty-two years. The old yellow and black 30 m.p.h. sign was replaced after about ten years when everything went metric. Man, and then another strange thing happened!

About two years after the event somebody else left a set of jerseys in their will to the club. I was talking to ou Jimmy from the garage after that and he tells me that the club has more jerseys than they can ever use. A lot of people seem to have died over the years. No, it's true, I tell you. Ou Jimmy does not tell tall stories.

Oh, yes, and just to show you what a good bloke ou Kallie was, I had to tell you.

Where was I now? Oh yes, back to the emergency meeting I was telling you about. Yes, because the road was was now finished and the families were preparing to move off into another direction, you follow! This would mean that eight blokes would not be here for the next season. What could be done to save rugby in Kuruman? That was the big question! Blitz Blignaut who played on the wing suggested it would be a good idea to blow up the road in many places. A few men nodded in silent approval, grinning. Groot Hendrik said that the best place would be in the big dip before the road turns off to Saltpeterpan. He might be able to get two sticks of dynamite from his uncle who had a blasting certificate and works on Modder B. He had always wanted to try his hand at blasting and would do the job if everybody was in favour. He did not want to do anything that the club thought was not right and might upset ou Kallie.

The president, ou Maxie, joined in the fun and thanked them for the possible solution to their problem but told them it could lead to a very ugly thing. They could all land up in the choekie and then there would be no players left anyway. Blitz said okay but he thought it would work. If ever they changed their minds they could talk to him about it later. Somebody said that they would not mind fetching the dynamite from Boksburg!

Apie the scrumhalf wanted to know when floods could be expected because he had heard that the people at the weather station had discovered new instruments that could tell them. Maxie thanked him for his input and reminded him that in the last fifty years there had never been floods here. Flip stated that he was ready to ask for his early pension and get a job with the municipality. His wife liked Kuruman, and that it was time to settle down. Klein Flippie was ready for school and had received his first little rugby ball from his oupa in Greylingstad.

Kallie had been very quiet sucking on his pipe, listening to the men talk. He now lit it, ordered another Klippies and water and reminded the men that the world was ruled by money. Everybody went silent and looked at him. They all ordered another drink. This could take a long time and be very interesting.

Kallie explained to them that if he as senior roads foreman could persuade the C.P.R.D. and also his brother-in-law at the P.W.D. in Kimberley to keep Kuruman as the base for future operations it would save the situation, as everybody was happy to stay in Kuruman. It would save the taxpayer a lot of money by not having to move everything to another place! The buildings and all the equipment cost a lot to move. The time was now ripe to talk to the authorities and he was the man to do it!

There was one problem, however. If Kuruman was kept as a base then everyone would have to be prepared to live in caravans and be away from home for a bit. They could come home for weekends. This was because he knew that the department was wanting to tar the Danielskuil road and wanted to move then to Postmasburg. Anyway it was worth a try. The men should go home and discuss it with their families. Everybody agreed loudly and some shouted "Hoor, hoor!" The meeting ended on a high note when Maxie put his hands in the till and bought them all a loopdop.

Now, as I have said before that if Kallie believed in something only the devil himself might knock him off his track for a while, you understand! Anyway he went home and Sannie knew straight away that he was facing another crisis and that he would tell her all in good time. That was his way, you know. He was a good husband and father.

The next day Kallie asked Elizabeth at the telephone exchange to get him the number of the M.P. for Vryburg and asked if he could come and discuss a very important issue with him. Yes, Kallie said, it had to do with politics. The member said he was too busy to see ou Kallie but could help him over the phone. Kallie said not to worry and said goodbye!

He then phoned the new young candidate who was standing against the member in the coming elections. The new outjie jumped at the chance and they all agreed to meet at Lykso after church on Sunday. Come the day and Kallie, Sannie, Kleinjan, Grietjie and Casper all went in his Hudson Terraplane with the white-walled tyres. It was all polished and shined up, I tell you! Kallie looked after his things, you know. That's why those yellow P.W.D. trucks and water carriers lasted so long.

Anyway, as Sannie explained to me later, Kallie was outstanding in his discussion with the National Party candidate. Sannie and the children stayed near the car, which was parked under a tree in the shade near the school. They had brought a flask of coffee and some rusks and lemonades with them, so they were happy to wait for ou Kallie. The candidate complimented her on her coffee as the two men kept talking under another tree. With his arm movements it looked as if Kallie was doing all the talking.

He told the candidate that to move people against their own free will was a sin as far as he was concerned. Each person had a right to choose their own future and enjoy good schooling for their children. He understood that work had to be done in the other areas but to have eight sad families in the department was a serious affair. It would be bad for the work as well.

Now, if he did not handle this whole affair very quickly and very quietly, it could have far-reaching effects on future departmental planning. This was especially so now that the election was just around the corner!

The candidate kept nodding his head as Kallie laid it on about Sunday schools, children crying, wives going back to their mothers and so on, you see! If he could, Kallie would make sure to collect as many votes for the M.P. as possible without overstepping the line as a government employee.

The lawyer was very pleased at this because he had heard all about Kallie before. Kallie strongly recommended that the candidate highlighted the savings of thousands of pounds of taxpayers' money by requesting the Roads Department in Kimberley to leave the Kuruman compound as it was. The lawyer was so enthralled by the logic behind it all that he promised his full co-operation to solve the Kuruman crisis!

Man, in any case, I don't know if you remember how close that election was. The young lawyer candidate took the trouble to follow up on Kallie's requests and kind of made Kuruman his favourite place for the time being, you follow? He spoke in the Town Hall and also visited the Skietkommando members. He mostly spoke about how bad it was to move people around as if they had no feelings. He was getting along with the people and they liked the way he stuck up for them. Fortunately the brother-in-law of Kallie in Kimberley could also see the clear picture and said a few good words to the groot kokkedore that counted. Well, my swaer, it all worked like a charm, as the Englishman says! Come election time and Kuruman was decorated with posters from here to Rhodesia, I tell you!

Oh, yes, I forgot to tell you that the big noises from the department visited the camp and Kuruman about six times and were entertained by the city fathers, so to say.

Well, they say that there were about four hundred registered voters in the Kuruman area and that the candidate won by 399 votes to become the new Member of Parliament! The one vote that could not count was because Oom Tollie died the night before.

The department decided to keep the depot in Kuruman there across the stream outside of the town and Kallie was promoted to area supervisor with an increase in salary. Hell, man, everybody was so happy that the whole dorp had a braaivleis at Die Oog, which started on a Friday and ended at midnight on the Saturday.

Now it also so happened that young Gysbert from Verlatenvlakte proposed to Elizabeth from the post office exchange and she accepted him, so it was a double celebration. What a time of the year this was! The start of a new rugby season, a proposal for marriage, a new Member of Parliament and the road depot to stay and grow bigger!

Oh, yes, it was also the wedding anniversary of Fanus and Lettie. Old Maxie Cohen again put his hand in his pocket and said he would pay for all the flowers for the wedding. The Royal Hotel was very busy, I tell you!

But man, guess what? I'm telling you that about a month later two parcels arrived in Kuruman. The one parcel had a full set of rugby jerseys and the other had socks and white pants in it. Nobody knew where they came from. They were addressed to:

Die Kuruman Rugbyklub,
P/A Kaapprovinsie Paddienste,
Kuruman
Noord Kaap

GREEN AND RED SOCKS

THERE WAS THIS HOTEL you see! The hotel was called The Royal and it was in Schweizer Reneke and it had the highest bar counter you have ever seen. I knew that the Western Transvaal had big blokes but this was something else, I tell you, boet! But now the funny thing was that they had the smallest bar boy you have put eyes on. His name was Meerkat, and he acted like one. Bliksem, it was funny! He kept vroeteling around the place, cleaning up, washing glasses, bringing in stock, running messages and so on. Every now and then he like pops up from behind the counter to see if everything was okay. He had to stand on a wooden crate to reach the shelves.

Anyway it was early in the afternoon—it was hot, dusty and ploegtyd in the district. I ordered a Coke because it seemed to be a popular drink, as most of the men were drinking it.

They really seemed to be enjoying it because they started to talk louder and louder the more they had. Only then did I see Meerkat replace the bottle of Klippies on the shelf. He hopped up onto his crate and broke the lid open with a flourish!

Oubaas Slyp Slabbert had khaki shorts on with veldskoene and old rugby socks on. These socks were not pulled up so only the red colour was seen. When he got up off his stoel to check if the cistern was working in the toilet only then did I see some green on the socks. I could see that the people were very loyal to the Western Transvaal here. I could see that because when they got hungry they got hot mielies and a slice of butter for a bar lunch. No, don't laugh. I'm telling the truth.

Now, Oom Slyp was very famous in this area because

he played front rank for the mielieboere for as long as anybody could remember. That is, if you remembered from just after the war to now. His eldest son was called Klein Slyp and his grandson Klein Klein Slyp and so on. The Oubaas got his name because he used to sluip around the scrums looking for scrumhalves and flyhalves, you know! There was a faded photo on the wall of a team in a frame, which Meerkat had to keep polished and clean at all times. Anyway, he was saying that in his day they used to have a thick red stripe across their green jerseys and red tops to their socks. Nowdays every blêrrie thing was changing.

He kept on about those green and red socks, you see. No more big, red top but now two bliksemse thin, red rings on the green. Anyhow, he sorted that problem out because Tant Clara has kept these socks together with a special wool for the last ten years or so. When he heard that the sports shop in Potch had twenty pairs left he bought the lot. Yes, there was a problem for the sub-union afterwards but my money was as good as any other person's, he said.

There was a new lightey serving and he thought he would make a big sale. You know how it is with these salespeople, mos? It was first come, first serve as the Englishman says. But now he had to borrow out some of them to the new boytjies with a threat of death if they were not washed and returned in good condition. He couldn't care a donder for these new socks. Even teams like Vrystaat, Grens and O.P. have two rings also, have you seen? What the hell! Now he remembers pushing against Boland just before the war and they had a gold top on their socks. That was the style. His old Springbok pal who he pushed against will agree. Two stripes is just a factory thing and all these young kokkedore in charge only think of blêrrie sales and not the feelings of people.

Ja, okay, thanks, maar dis nou die loopdop! Also thinking about the costs gives me the stuipe. Today's outjies want petrol money and say it is too far to come to practice. In my day I used to ploeg all day on Fridays and then drive my John Deere twenty-five miles to practice. It was a problem because my togs were covered in sand and dust because the toolbox behind the seat had no lid. Witbooi broke the blêrrie thing off one day. On my way back to the farm with my lights on my neighbours knew I had been to practice, my maat.

Yes, yes, I know—I once missed the farm turnoff. It was late at night on that Wolmaranstad road and I ran out of diesel. It was no problem because I gets a lift to my road with Spanner's donkey cart who was going for a Transvaal roadworthy test early in the morning. I never did agree with that new donderse law. Ja, ja—kak en betaal, is die wet van Transvaal, as we says around here.

As I was saying. Ag, ja, Clara was so worried that night that she phoned the ouderling and reported me missing, John Deere and all! I still had my togs and socks on.

Now our ouderling told Clara about the Good Samaritan and this calmed her down a bit, she told me. She accepted his advice and started to bake vetkoek and porridge for breakfast.

By this time, our nommer-asseblief lady at the

sentrale came on duty at halfses the morning and heard that I was missing. This all came about because Neels from Ottosdal wanted to know if I had had any rain. We all phoned each other early in the morning before the farm lines got too busy. Neelsie was so upset that he called out the Ottosdal Commando! He could do this quickly because his eldest daughter Elfrida was on the exchange and accepted no calls during an emergency. His instructions were clear. Horse, biltong, dried peaches, rusks, rifle and ammunition for a week and meet at Sandfontein in six hours' time. If somebody was looking for a wapenskou they would get it. Maybe some uitlanders were up to their tricks again. A friend is a friend, you understand, he used to say.

Anyway, now, I was walking the ten miles to the farm when there was this donderslag and the heavens opened up. Rain, my swaer, you cannot believe it! I always wanted to make a better drift over the Droogspruit but you know how it is. The spruit was running so strongly that I had to wait under the willowtree close by. I was wet, hungry and all brommed up, you understand. As the sun was coming up I saw the farmhouse three miles away. I knew Clara was waiting for me because I could see the smoke from the kitchen chimney. I crossed the spruit farther up.

Clara was so pleased to see me that she wanted to phone the ouderling immediately. The telephone line was down and those vetkoeke were lovely. After the eats I put my togs in the oven to dry out for the game. I had to saddle up ou Kroon later to get to town in time for the game.

Now, we were playing Wolmaranstad at Schweizer,

a derby day as the Engelsman says. They came over in a helse big school bus with a cooking radiator. They were all singing en groot menere, you know. The game was at the showgrounds. You know where all those bloekombome are now, and those sinkplaathokkies ... well there was the place! The visitors were well organized as they could change in the bus and leave their clothes there. Some of them came dressed ready for the game but carried a pair of shoes with them for afterwards, you understand. That was because they could not dance nicely in their boots at the dance later.

We had to go behind the trees to get into our rugby togs and they were not so big then. Ja, thanks, ou Meerkat knows what I likes. Ja, where was I? Ja nee, as I was saying ... the ref was ou Corrie, the postmaster, who was a tennis player. His white tekkies could be seen by all of us. He borrowed the whistle from the stationmaster who would not need it because there were no trains on a Saturday or Sunday. Do you remember when a stationmaster put out a green flag and blew his whistle? You kissed koebaai quickly and waved sakdoekies. He also had a ring around his arm for the guardsvan guard to catch on the way through the station. I think it was to do with a key to unlock points, or something like that.

In elk geval, from behind the third bloekomboom we saw a lot of spectators sitting on chairs borrowed from the hotel. Oh, yes, the field was marked with chalk that morning. This was given to the Rugby Club and the showgrounds by the Roads Department. You know, they ordered four bags and got forty. Some English clerk in Klerksdorp made a mistake and we have to pay taxes for those blêrrie mistakes, you know.

Corrie the postmaster blew on the railway whistle from the middle of the field to let us know that he was ready. Wolmaranstad ran from the bus and all their followers cheered. We ran from the trees in a straight stripe, some swinging their arms to loosen up. The ref was about to start the game when Spanner's roadworthy cart crossed the field, pulled by two slow donkeys. Jonas, the driver gave me a thumbs-up sign and grinned with his haasbek. Now I knows donkeys are stupid and so are Jonas.

But thinking twice, Jonas was correct because the shortcut to the road was across the field. It had a helse middelmannetjie that cut through the middle line. I told him to go but he wanted to show me the four Leghorn hens and a black Austrolop rooster he had bought for five shillings, hok and all. Dolf from the P.W.D. shouted that he should try a carrot! Stupid, hey? Carrots were scarce and all the shops were closed.

Nee, nee, my magtig, goeie genugtig. Okay, then and that is the loopdop. Thanks hey! Nou ja, the ref stands on the middelmannetjie and Jonas disappeared slowly towards the road. The ref blew on his whistle again, the rooster in the cage crowed and we charged. The ref got a fright and twisted his ankle and fell down. We all stood like children around him as he was moaning and holding his ankle. The fluitjie was bitten by his teeth and was still in his mouth. Wolmaranstad couldn't care and picked up the ball and scored a try. We all saw that it was a knock on! Ou Corrie saw nothing and lay on his back with his leg in the air. We thought that he would be orraait but he was hurt. Meanwhile they missed the conversion from under the posts.

The next person with authority was the ouderling and all thirty supporters looked towards him. My old oupa used to say that a man is a man when called upon in a minute! Like Majuba, he also used to say. With a nervous cough he stood up and removed his tie. He took his jacket off and trotted onto the field and took the whistle from ou Corrie who was being carried off. The new ref had black shoes on but after a while they were a mixture of brown dust and white chalk. He was a Western Province man and knew his rules. He also knew the Bible very well. Like for instance after the first scrum he gave a vryskop against me and asked me what the Moses I was doing and did I think I was Goliath?

In any case, oh yes, I never liked Dries from Wolmaranstad because he had his eye on my Clara when we were much younger. Now it was on our twenty-five with a minute or so to go and we were still three nil down. That was according to their score, you understand. But we knew that there was no score at all. We had a scrum and I pushes down and puts his nose into the white chalk. It was like stikstof because he stikked and coughed. The ouderling blew his whistle and gave them another bliksemse penalty!

Dries stood up and blew his nose on his sleeve. He looked at me and if he had a gun I think he would have shot me. Now Dries was the captain and decided to have his revenge and take the kick himself. Where did you see that a bloke like Dries could kick? I knew he had a new pair of whalebone-tip boots on for kickers. My heart was in my dust-covered boots as I looked across towards Clara. She looked so small and timid with her golden hair shining and her hands clasped together on her lap.

Dries placed the ball and took five steps back, pulled up his pants, just like another Springbok from Transvaal I pushed against. Everybody was kop onderstebo and quiet as we watched Dries. Just then the Ottosdal Commando charged through the trees firing their Lee Metfords and Mausers into the air as the dust flew everywhere. They were shouting, "Waar is Slyp, waar is Slyp?"

Dries lost his nerve and with a woer-woer kick he hit the upright below the crossbar. He fell to the ground with a pulled muscle in his leg. Ouderling blew his whistle and walked upright with his nose in the air so to speak as the commando rode around shouting. You see they also used this ground for training sometimes.

We all trooped off to the hotel for a bath and a drink. Ag, hell, today it is Ellis Park, Nuweland, Springbok Park, Boet Erasmus, Loftus, King's Park, Olen, B.R.U., Pam Brink and all those others. But to us our field was always known as 'The Veld'.

PIRATES OF THE TRANSKEI

THE ROYAL HOTEL WAS the headquarters of the famous Pirates Rugby Club in Umtata. The area was then known as the Transkei Territories and teams from Butterworth, Idutywa, Umtata, Engcobo, Maclear, Elliot and Ugie battled it out for the Benning Cup year after year.

Traditional Friday nights saw the place crowded with members of both the rugby and cricket sides playing darts and swopping yarns. Some were good at darts while others just came along for the jol. You found that the company reps were usually the best players because they played every night at the hotels in the towns where they did business.

Anyway the Pirates had supporters and members throughout the territory in those days. Therefore what the Pirates lacked in ability, on the rare occasion they made up for it in spirit. They had a good cross-section of members, which included traders from the more rural areas as well. Many of these men had sons at the three great rugby schools of the Border namely—Dale College of Kingwilliamstown, Selborne College of East London and Queens College of Queenstown. When these boys came home from boarding school they often found themselves thrust into the town side.

Pirates took their rugby seriously and played a bright, open, running game while the other Umtata side, called the Rec Club, played a good, hard, basic style. These two clubs were great rivals and the Rec also had a large following of supporters. The derby-day clashes between these two rivals were always great, festive occasions. The stand was festooned with the black and white colours of the Pirates and the red and black colours of the Rec. The stand was split in half for the spectators' seating and much banter went on, as you can imagine.

Now the strange thing about these two rival sides were the jerseys they wore and their style of play. Pirates had identical colours to Natal while Rec were the same as Eastern Province. The large majority of the Rec players were from the Afrikaans community while the Pirates attracted the English-speaking community. As it happened the derby days always had a bit of needle in them. The Rec had members from the government services, S.A.R. & H., Forestry and the like.

Anyway, this particular derby-day week started in spectacular fashion for the Pirates. Their young flank forward who was celebrating his coming of age at the hotel in Elliotdale fell through the bar floor while doing a Zulu war dance. He sprained his ankle but also discovered a case of rare whisky that had been hidden under the floor for about twenty years. For over three weeks the patrons had to walk around a large gaping hole in front of the counter. The next day was Sunday and it was the Pirates' annual golf day at the country club. Regular players teed off first so as to let the fancy-dressed players have their moments of glory swarming all over the rough.

One player did have his moment of sheer glory and it happened like this. It was at the short eleventh, which was a par three, 101 yarder, well bunkered with the out-of-bounds fence only ten yards on the other side of the green. In the private property there was a corrugated-iron long-drop toilet situated about five yards from the boundary fence separating the two areas. Yes, you guessed what would happen, and happen it did, you can ask Sarge about it!

Ou Van, the lock forward, hit the ball with great gusto and hopelessly overclubbed. The ball screamed off the tee and hit the back of the corrugated-iron toilet with a resounding clatter. This rifle-shot sound was followed by a startled bellow from within. The next moment the local police sergeant came hopping out through the door like a kangaroo. He was holding on to his pants with his left hand and still clutching his Sunday newspaper with the other, his Sherlock Holmes pipe still clutched between his teeth!

He was a staunch Pirates supporter but shouted that he would resign if this had anything to do with that fourball. He was going to attend the prizegiving that evening but now he was not so sure anymore. He wanted to know who had done the nasty deed but the players just looked at each other and, laughing and holding their stomachs, sank to their knees. Sarge did attend the evening function but cast a wary eye around for any leaks on the incident. Throughout the week people were talking about the loud noise from the hill near the golf course.

Now it was the Friday night before the game and the Pirates players and some supporters all gathered at the headquarters to discuss matters of importance. One very staunch supporter was a middle-aged factory representative and had spent all week calling on his customers in the bundu. His wife had given him strict instructions to proceed direct to East London, as she would be waiting for him at the in-laws' place prior to going on holiday to the Cape. She had locked up the house in Umtata, reported the matter to the police and asked them to keep an eye on the place for a couple of weeks. She had taken the family car to East London, as Terry wanted his N.D.-registered company car to go in for a major service at the agents in East London while they were on holiday.

Anyway, as things would happen our friend got a bit carried away and was deep into rugby talk when he suddenly realized what the time was. He dashed to the phone and phoned Babs his wife in East London. After a broadside salvo from her it was decided that he should come down early the next morning. All was now okay and he returned to the gathering all smiles.

Later that night our friend returned home in a not-so-stable condition and had difficulty in finding his back-door key, which was on his key ring. He eventually found it but had a problem sticking it into the slot. He was still battling with this operation when a firm hand informed him that he was under arrest for attempted housebreaking and trespassing. No amount of protesting could sway the new constable from his first arrest. The constable also noticed that the registration of the car in the driveway was N.D. and not the C.C.Y. of Umtata.

Under escort by the policeman and with wavering step he decided to go along with the Law and was helped into the back of the local pick-up van called the 'Black Maria'. The trip to the local police station took only a few minutes and with a squeak of brakes the van stopped in the yard of the copshop. With a flair for efficiency the constable unlatched the back door and tried to help our buddy out. He climbed out by himself and shrugged off any form of assistance.

Now the sergeant on duty was the same oke who'd had his Sunday reading interrupted in the toilet the previous Sunday. Anyway, he was busy going through some complaints about someone letting down the tyres of all the cars parked in front of the Royal Hotel that night. He told me that at that moment his mind was on the time he pushed against Moff at the Police Academy in Pretoria. All of a sudden a suspect and the arresting constable were standing in front of his desk.

Sarge looked up and clasped his head in his hands and stared at the desk. After a while he reached for his cold cup of coffee and let out a sigh. Terry was now standing all humble-like with his hands clasped in front of him like a person going up for communion. Now our buddy had been in this position before. He was once an able bodied seaman serving on His Majesty's corvettes during the war and had reported back late on board one night at Chatham.

What seemed like an age Sarge told them to sit down and tell him all about it. The constable started his report while Terry was becoming D.D.M.I.—'Dik die moer in'. In good English it means, highly agitated. The suspect objected to being arrested in his own yard after parking his car on *his* flowerbed. The constable counteracted by saying that the N.D. registration was sufficient for him, with the assumption that this was a tresspassing case with intent to housebreaking as well!

Now, Sarge was a man of depth and took time to make a decision. He lit his pipe and with a large puff decided to go to the toilet. The constable and the suspect were now enveloped in a cloak of silence with nothing more to say. Ou Sarge came back feeling much better but first had to answer a telephone call about a complaint of a barking dog.

Sarge then made his decision. The suspect was to be returned to his home immediately. A false arrest had been made. This entitled the suspect to sit in front of the van while being taken back to the place of unlawful arrest. A pat on the back for the new constable for vigilance shown and for reading the request book. Tonight he was on duty, but tomorrow was derby day! Everybody was satisfied.

On Saturday morning the town was treated to a cavalcade of cars manned by Pirates supporters. On the back of an open truck some gallows had been erected from which hung a stuffed Rec jersey. Somebody was dressed in a sackcloth robe with a mask on and ringing a bell next to the gallows. There were shouts and jeers from the people in town, all clapping hands and laughing and having a hell of a time. Young quedines ran next to the gallows truck shouting in delight as only children can do. The traffic cop was also all smiles for a change as he conducted affairs on his Norton from the lead position at the front of the procession.

As a show of unity the Pirates supporters peeled off and headed for the Royal to discuss matters a bit further. The execution vehicle turned off and made its way to the Imperial Hotel, which was the Rec headquarters. The effigy was promptly offloaded and carried into the bar, gallows and all. Bennie the barman was a bit surprised because he raised his right eyebrow by about a sixteenth of an inch.

This supporting gang was now joined by anybody who was getting into the swing of things, so to speak. Laughter and great humour prevailed, which tended to get louder and louder with the arrival of more Rec supporters. Paddy, the Irishman, who was the owner of the hotel was a perfect host and rolled up his sleeves and helped Bennie who was taking pressure in keeping up with the orders from the patrons. The local fire chief, also a Paddy, arrived with the intention of checking for fire hazards and enquiring whether all the hoses and hydrants were in working order.

Meanwhile back at the Royal the Pirates hierarchy was plotting the downfall of the Rec side. The entire team was taken through to the big lounge and sat on the edges of the bamboo chairs and listened to the president's pep talk.

The players left quietly for home to check if the maids had ironed their jerseys and shorts. One of the instructions from the president was that no player should have a large lunch the following day. A trader from the Tsolo district protested that he had not eaten for a week. The president reminded him that he was not a player but an executive member. This had a calming effect on him because he ordered another beer.

The Municipal Recreation Ground was the home of the Transkei Rugby Union and the one turnstile was manned by old man Roy from the Town Council Treasury Department. He always brought a ticket-holder contraption with him to accommodate the two-shilling, pink ticket rolls. Scholars had to pay sixpence and babes in arms were free. On the open side of the field cars were allowed to park along a white line six foot from the touchline.

Now back to the day of the game. With the stands full and buzzing the referee from Elliot arrived amidst a few hushed claps. It was remembered by some diehards that during a previous game he controlled he had a problem in keeping up with the play and kept using his whistle to bring it back to him. Or so the story goes. He was extremely upset when he heard a local calling him a horse thief, as he was a speculator by profession. By this time old Roy suggested that the ref should pay the two-bob entrance fee! The ref threatened to take the matter up at the next T.R.U. executive meeting scheduled for that same evening, so old Roy relented and muttered something about refs with no sense of humour and no sense as well.

In the Pirates' dressing room all was abuzz and Billy, the Pirates captain, insisted that Ringo the scrumhalf pull one of his chest hairs out for good luck. This was done with glee but a howl followed as more than one was wrenched from his extended chest. There was a smell of Wintergreen ointment everywhere, then Fred the lock had to dash away to his car because he had forgotten his boots.

Colleen, a player's wife, had knitted Pirates jerseys for their twin boys. The two four-year-old boys ran onto the field and dropped the ball near the centre spot. The Pirate half of the stand went wild. Pirates ran onto the field followed by loud cheering as the Rec team made their appearance. The play was hard and fast with the Pirates running the ball at every opportunity. From his centre position Sarge Wilson kept on urging the forwards for more ball. The Pirate scrumhalf and his eighth man worked a perfect dummy close to the line and Billy crashed over under the posts for the first try of many that day.

This was the signal for the floodgates to open as the Natal-jerseyed Pirates climbed in good and proper as they say. The half-time whistle sounded and the players trooped off towards their trays of orange slices and bottles of water. The ref took a piece from each tray just to show that he was unbiased!

The second half was a repeat of the first. There was a scrum near the touchline on the open side and Gibby, the Pirates frontranker, was blown up for lifting. He, however, kept on heaving upwards into his opposition and another shrill blast on the whistle calmed him down. The ref called him aside and started to lecture him. He explained to the ref that because of all the blowing hooters, he had not heard the whistle blow. He seemed to have gone deaf. The red-faced ref immediately paced off another ten yards and pointed to the posts.

Would the Rec side now get onto the scoreboard? Their kick hit the upright and sliced into the arms of the Pirates left wing who started to run. A linking movement began inside the Pirates' twenty-five and the ball went wide, which resulted in a spectacular try. Gibby mentioned to the ref that every dog gets his day. The end whistle blew with Pirates running out clear winners with a twenty-five-point margin. A record against their old foes. Handshakes all round by the players as they trooped off to the cold showers.

The players dived into the showers with zest and

hurriedly changed into their club blazers and ties and headed for the Imperial Hotel because Rec were the hosts that year. Wives and girlfriends joined the players in the guest lounge adjoining the main bar as no females were allowed into bars in those days. The party began modestly with the captains making speeches, thanking the opposition team for the game and the spirit in which it was played. As the evening progressed the players disappeared into the main bar to be with friends and supporters. One by one the ladies left with promises from their men that they would be home shortly etc. etc. etc.!

Paddy the owner was on the ball as more and more snacks arrived from the kitchen. By now the three barmen were extended to the limit as thirsty men called for service. The Pirates got together and sang their song:

> *We are Pirates*
> *We are Pirates*
> *We're a long way from home*
> *And if you don't like us*
> *Just leave us alone*

> *We drink when we're thirsty*
> *We drink when we're dry*
> *We run with the ball*
> *And score another try*
> *For the Pirates Club we'll die!*

> *P. I. R. A. T. E. S. ... Pirates!*

By now ties and jackets had been removed and laughter and jokes were the order of the day. The celebrations were going into top gear. Colin, the Pirate right wing, complained that he could not see out of his black eye. Someone suggested that he got himself a black patch like Long John Silver. He replied that he had never played against him and where was he from?

About ten o'clock whispers were heard that Teuns, the Rec captian, had met with a fatal car accident on the way to Viedgesville. Everybody was dumbfounded and spoke in low tones and looked around for his brother who was also missing. Everything now seemed different as men stood around not really knowing what to do next.

Slowly the batwing doors, which led onto the verandah, opened gently and a coffin was carried in by six Rec supporters all with long faces. You could have heard a pin drop as the patrons stared aghast at the procession. The coffin was gently lowered to the floor and the six pallbearers headed for the bar. Everybody stood still and not a word was spoken. Some blokes swallowed hard and stopped sipping their beer. Others shook their heads and suggested that this was probably the way to go.

The local undertaker, Vernon, who was a Rec supporter, suggested that the Pirates should come forward and pay their last respects to their Theunsie. Somebody pushed Billy the captain forward to lead the procession of Pirates, but he in turn pushed Ringo the scrumhalf ahead who swallowed hard and tiptoed towards the closed coffin, followed by the team.

The bar was by now very quiet and somebody

muffled his cough. All eyes were riveted on the coffin as the Pirates approached as silently as they could. Suddenly the lid flew open and Theuns, resplendent in his rugby jersey, sat bolt upright and shouted, "Whaaaa!" The recoiling of Pirates was instantaneous as bodies bumped into each other in the scramble to get away from the coffin! Gertjie slipped and cut his head on the floor and muttered that his medical aid would never pay for that. A thunderous applause by the Rec supporters echoed down the empty streets of Umtata. They had got their own back in spectacular fashion.

Theuns was still in the coffin and enjoying himself with a beer in each hand, donated by Pirates. The Pirates looked sheepishly at one another and burst out laughing in sheer relief. Cisco the hooker lamented that the buggers must never do a thing like that again. Owen nodded his head in total agreement while Colin decided not to motor back to Qumbu that evening.

Still visibly shaken by it all, the Pirate contingent turned and headed back to the counter to be met by wide grins from the barmen. The effect of this bizarre counterattack had to be overcome immediately and another drink could do just that. The noise and banter started all over again.

"Last round, please, gentlemen," was repeated many times before everybody decided that enough was enough. Private parties were formed as players and supporters decided that they must share this experience with family and friends at home. One irate wife chased her husband's guests away upon arrival at his house. Many a wife had to get out of bed and serve food to starving, uninvited guests.

Umtata had just experienced one of those great after-derby-day parties. The *Transkei Territorial News* had a lot to say in its rugby column the following Friday. Sadly to say, these two great rival clubs are no longer in existence. It was a great period to remember.

At 2.30 a.m. Umtata slumbered peacefully again with the blue lamp from the police station shining brightly.

DIE BUFFEL VAN DEWETSDORP

MANY YEARS AGO THEY had a rugby team in this town. They always had their meetings at the old Royal Hotel. It was over there but it is now a big shop as you can see. I am old now but I used to take the municipality's post to the post office every afternoon. Many times there was no post but I was allowed to sit here under the Town Clerk's window. I still get my tea every morning and afternoon in that special big jam tin with a handle on it. Baas Boetie had it put on for me by Oubaas Jannie who was a blacksmith but has died a long time ago.

When some of the Town Clerk's people have a birthday then I also get some lekker cake. I also had to wash cars sometimes after it had rained because they had a lot of mud on them. Yes, I still get paid every month and I am very happy and still do work here. I now live in the new location and have a good bicycle. I also take messages to people and buy things for the staff at the café and co-op. I can also water the plants and pull out the weeds.

Now I first saw this game of rugby played when I was very young. I think it was when there was a great war overseas and General de Wet was put into gaol by General Smuts.

They used to play at the old showgrounds over there and it was very dusty and dry in winter. On that day Baas Buffel Bester from Buffelsfontein played very hard and his jersey was badly torn by some Wepener player. After the game he saw me standing next to the zinc shed and threw me that black and white jersey. It

72

was so warm that I put it around my shoulders to keep the cold out.

I followed behind the people at a distance so that they would not see me near the hotel. I sat under the window of the bathroom and watched the steam coming out. There was much singing and laughter. Everybody was so happy. It was strange to me because I saw somebody wiping blood from his nose and another player hopping off the field on one leg. Somebody patted him on his shoulder and he stumbled. They then helped him to his car. He was not angry but smiled and thanked them all.

Many important people watched that match. The postmaster was there. My mother used to work for them. The man from the bank was there as well as the stationmaster. I did not like that stationmaster because he was always dressed in black and never smiled. He always had a big silver badge on his pocket. I must tell you that he got very excited and was always shouting at the players and telling them what to do.

Yes, I lived with my mother in the location and she was never angry with me for coming home a little bit late on a Saturday after a game. She knew that I was a good son because I was going to school at the mission station just outside of the town. The priests used to tell us what was right and what was wrong in this life.

Now that jersey Baas Buffel gave me was so big that I could put my feet and legs into the sleeves and sleep like that. It made me warm on my straw mat. Sometimes my mother wanted to wash it and I always had to hang it up in the sun so that I could use it again that night.

After the Sunday school lessons I would walk into

town to see all the cars around the big church. I often saw Baas Buffel with his big black car that had white tyres. He was very important because he always talked to everybody and they listened. His wife was always with him and also his two children. They were about my age. One was a boy and the other a girl. The boy had black hair like Baas Buffel and the girl had golden hair like Madam Tienie.

My mother told me that when I went into town I had to be polite and greet people. Another thing my mother told me was that I must never have a snotneus as this really upset people. I was not to join naughty children and hang around shop doors or sit on the steps of the post office. That was because a lot of people came to the post office and she did not want me to look like a little loafer.

Now I remember the day that changed my life. It was at a rugby game. On that Saturday a team from Bloemfontein came to Dewetsdorp to play against Baas Buffel. They had white jerseys with red collars. After the game those white jerseys were the colour of the showground sand. I followed all the cars from the Royal to the field. I went to the other side of the field, away from all the people and sat on my jersey under the bluegum trees. There was also another man there in grey flannels and a tie. He asked me please to fetch the ball if it was kicked out on that side of the field. He would wave a handkerchief when the ball was out of play and the players would listen to him and line up in a straight stripe. Somebody would throw the ball in and they would wrestle for it.

All of a sudden somebody fell down and lay very

still in the sand. The players all stood around him and did nothing. I saw that it was Baas Buffel and got a big fright. I remembered that my mother told me that if anybody fell down and lay very still you have to cover him up with something to keep warm. I was scared but ran onto the field and ducked in between the big men and spread my jersey over Baas Buffel. I was sure it would keep him warm. I ran back to the small hill near the bluegums and watched on my stomach.

The stationmaster ran onto the field carrying a bucket of water and shouting orders. Another man was pumping Baas Buffel's legs onto his chest. Some water was thrown onto his face and he sat up shaking his head and wiping his face with his sleeve. He was okay. Baas Buffel then saw the jersey over his legs, which he folded up and placed next to the field. I did not know what to do, so I stayed where I was. Later I ran down and picked up my jersey and ran back to my hiding place.

Some time later the cars blew their hooters, the people clapped and everybody went back to the hotel. Dewetsdorp lost the game, I remember. Peeping through the hotel window I saw everybody shouting and clapping as Baas Buffel swallowed a beer quickly. The men were singing, "Hy lyk vir my so baie na 'n koek se hoenderhaan!" They sang that over and over again.

Now after school the following Wednesday I went into town and waited for my friend Sheshi. We would play klippies in the sand and watch the horses and cars go by. We were busy playing when all of a sudden a big shadow fell across us. We looked up startled and saw

Baas Buffel standing over us with his hands behind his back. Man, I got scared and pulled my jersey over my shoulders. He laughed softly and gave me a parcel wrapped in brown paper and string.

He asked me my name and why I had put that jersey over him as he lay on the ground.

I stammered, "Baas, my mother told me that men lying in the veld could get cold and needed warmth." I saw Sheshi standing around the corner picking his nose and watching us. The big man told me to open the packet, which I did with trembling hands. It was a brand-new rugby jersey, so thick and shiny. It smelled so new and clean! I was shy and whispered a 'baie dankie, my baas'.

He then sat down on his haunches next to me and asked me if I wanted him to be my baas. I sommer said yes, straight away. I was so very happy! It was then that my mother had to look after his dorpshuis and we moved into beautiful rooms at the bottom of the garden. The postmaster's wife was so kind to my mother and also gave her a new tea-set After I got my Standard Five at the mission I was put in charge of sheep and cattle on Buffelsfontein. I got well paid by Baas Buffel and I was a man.

I also learned to drive a John Deere and went to farmers' shows in Harrismith, Bloemfontein and a big one on the Reef near Johannesburg. This was over the Easter time.

Bethlehem was very cold and I did not like it there during the shows. Kleinbaas Gertjie and I used to go horse riding together and chase each other across the vlakte shouting with the wind in our faces. It was very nice! They all called me Klonkie and I was known all over the area as that.

Baas Buffel and Miesies Tienie now live in town. Kleinbaas Gertjie, also known as Klein Buffel, and his family now live on the farm. Kleinnooi Tienie married a magistrate and they now live in Bethal in the Transvaal. I am back in the garden room at Baas Buffel's townhouse. Baas Buffel got me a job with the municipality so that I could watch rugby on Saturday afternoons and sit in the sun in my old age. My mother died many years ago and I never took a wife.

Baas Buffel died aged ninety-two and Tienie passed away a year later. Klonkie was still alive at age seventy-five.

OPERATION OSTRICH

MAN, YOU KNOW, SOMETIMES the game can have a funny time as well. I will tell you what happened in a game between Hartley and Gatooma just after the war. A Scot by the name of Jock came out to visit some relatives and somehow got a game on the wing for us. I think we were one bloke short and drafted him in chop-chop to fill the side. They said he was very fast when somebody was chasing him. I think our wing was away hunting in the Kalahari at that time.

Anyway, in those days the wing threw the ball in at the lineouts. Our team had a special call as to where the ball should be thrown into the lineout. For example, if the name of an animal was called out then the ball would be thrown to the back half of the lineout. If the name of a bird was called out by the scrumhalf then the ball would be thrown to the front half of the lineout. Understand, hey?

Well, it was our lineout and Jock was coping pretty well so far. He stood with the ball waiting for the call. Ou Freddy forgot that Jock could not understand Afrikaans and called "Volstruis!"

The furrows on Jock's brow got deeper as he started to think about the call. He walked over to Freddy and asked, "Hell, mon, what was that you called?"

Freddy looked around and whispered, "Ostrich!"

The lineout men got ready again as Jock walked back to his position. He stopped short of it, turned around and walked back to Freddy. The lineout men relaxed again and looked at each other. The ref started to look bedonderd and glanced at his watch. What for I don't know!

Ou Jock whispered to Freddy and asked, "Is it an animal or a bird?"

Freddy was not sure and called Tommy our fullback to sort out the problem. He came trotting up from fullback to join the conference just as the ref blew very hard on his whistle and awarded Gatooma a penalty for us delaying play on purpose. I ask you, with tears in my eyes!

The lineout was near our blêrrie line and the scores were level with a few minutes of play left. The bloke slotted the penalty and that was that. He was a good player and used to play for Matabeleland and Rhodesia. Poor old Jock was so upset at the Royal afterwards that he kept telling everybody that he was going to stick to soccer in future as this bloody game was for the animals and the birds and that he had pulled a muscle as well.

JACK THE HOOTERS

THERE WAS A PERIOD when a game between the mines Simmer & Jack and E.R.P.M. (East Rand Premier Mine), known as the 'Hooters', was a tough affair. There was this one game played at Boksburg that was no different from the others except that after a fist flew in a scrum and a Jack stayed down it ended in laughter.

It happened like this. The game I think was on a knife's edge at two penalties apiece and time was running out. The scrum went down with the front rankers charging at each other while the ref ran around to the other side to see if the ball was being put in straight. Gert saw his chance and sent a piledriver uppercut onto the chin of ou Ernest. Hooters hooked the ball quickly and it was booted into touch.

The forwards straggled towards the lineout, shirts hanging out and all that. They were damn tired, I could see. Somebody noticed Ernest sitting in the middle of the field shaking his head and wiping a bloody nose. He stumbled onto his feet and walked towards the lineout rolling up his sleeves. He took in his position next to Gert, rolled up his sleeves even further ... with murder in his eyes.

Two young schoolboys were fighting over who would give the ball back to the wing to throw in.

Ernest growled aloud, "What's the blêrrie delay?" He was told that the ball was still coming. "Bugger the bliksemse ball. Let's get on with the game!" He then barged Gert right off his feet as he was still in the air.

The ref went bananas and sent them both off ... one to each side of the field to cool off. When the final whistle blew the ref called them together, and grinning sheepishly they shook hands with each other. They were the last to leave the club that night. Both won higher rugby honours later that year and became great friends.

BOXING NOT ALLOWED

I THINK THAT THE Hamilton Club of East London in the Border area created a world record by having two players sent off at the same time while no play was taking place. This is how it happened. First of all you must realize that this club had produced more Border and Springbok players than all the other clubs combined. It was a real rugby club. They were highly competitive and even the lower sides were stacked with older, experienced players ... on their way down, so to say.

So, on this particular day, I think they were playing against Cambridge on the B.R.U. No. 2 field, next to the main ground. This was a third league game and both sides were high up on the log. Anyway, Cambridge ran in a try under the Hams' posts and the conversion was about to take place when it all happened. As the Cambridge flyhalf was about to place the ball a brawl started behind the posts.

There were two Hamilton players slugging it out with fists up and dancing around, throwing punches at each other right behind the posts. They were blaming each other for not tackling the try scorer. The flabbergasted ref, old Dad as everybody called him, was not sure what to do, so he ran into the mêlée blowing on his whistle and shouting at them to stop. He then slipped and fell on his arse. Everybody packed down with laughter but he kept blowing on his whistle from a sitting position with his arm held high.

The Cambridge side decided to sit down on the halfway line and watch the entertainment from afar.

The lonely kicker, who was still waiting to convert the ball, also took a breather. At last Dad regained his composure, dusted himself off and gave another blast on the whistle. Both pugilists got a tongue-lashing and their marching orders amidst a flurry of arms. Dad pointed dramatically towards the main stand where the dressing rooms were and another game in progress on the 'A' field. Spectators on the main grandstand were at a loss as to why two Hams players were making their way to the dressing rooms in front of them.

The kick was missed the first time but Dad gave them another shot at the poles because there were two infringements. I think that the two okes got a two-match suspension from the Border Rugby Union, which they accepted by grinning and shaking hands before the disiplinary committee.

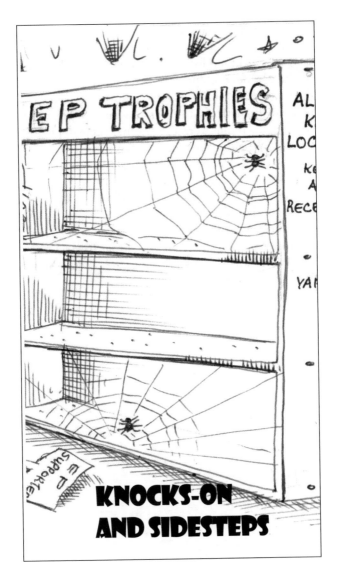

KNOCKS-ON
AND SIDESTEPS

A G.R.I. (GERMISTON RAILWAY INSTITUTE) team arrived to play Unicorn in Boksburg with only thirteen men. The rival skipper offered to lend them a couple of players from the stand, but the G.R.I. captain replied, "Thanks, but no ou bees (old ox), we won't be two short, too long!"

$$🏉🏉🏉🏉🏉$$

Heard the one about the Eastern Province coach who at a coaching session clapped his hands and shouted, "Okay boys, take up your normal positions!"

The players all went and stood behind the tryline!

$$🏉🏉🏉🏉🏉$$

Overheard at a match between a Durban and Johannesburg side at King's Park while two men with distinctive Indian accents were having an argument:

"No, man, that is being not so, I telling you!"

"My good golly man, where you from?"

"Parkview!"

"Well park you too man!"

$$🏉🏉🏉🏉🏉$$

One of the big lumbering forwards from Heidelberg in the Transvaal, following up a kick ahead, tackled the opposing fullback after the latter had kicked the ball into touch. The referee immediately blew his whistle and awarded a penalty and called the offender nearer.

"What's that for Mr. Ref?"

"A blêrrie late tackle, that's what!"

"Okay, but I could not get there any earlier!"

🏉🏉🏉🏉🏉

Once, during a rather uninspiring and exasperating match on the Gnoll Ground in Neath, one regular turned to his pal and said, "Dai, I've seen better wings on chickens!"

To which Bryn replied in mournful tones, "Aye, Dai, and better centres in chocolates."

🏉🏉🏉🏉🏉

A top-class student from Tukkies (Pretoria University) played a game for his hometown of Delareyville in the Western Transvaal against a side from Sannieshof during his mid-year holidays. He received the ball from a set scrum, beat his opposite number with a dazzling spurt of speed and a perfect dummy and repeated his trick on the wrong-footed fullback to score under the posts.

With disbelief he looked back and saw the referee awarding a penalty against him on the spot where he had sold his first dummy.

With hands on hips he softly remarked to the ref that his decision was rather unusual, and received the reply, "We don't want any big-city, show-off stuff like that on the platteland ... if you're going to pass the blêrrie ball, then pass the blêrrie thing!"

🏉🏉🏉🏉🏉

A local optometrist was once asked to referee a game between Standerton and Volksrust. He was rather small of stature and was twice bowled over by a huge flank from the visiting Standerton side. On neither occasion was there an apology forthcoming from the player. Just before the final whistle the same forward hurled himself over the line for what would have been the winning try. It was turned down because of a forward pass.

The panting forward was enraged and shouted at the ref, "My bliksem, ref, you need a blêrrie pair of specs with thick glasses!"

The little ref looked up at him and calmly replied, "You're the blindside forward, not me."

🏉🏉🏉🏉🏉

At a Villagers' home game in Cape Town the referee was continually under fire from a certain section of the crowd, who were of the opinion that he was failing to see the mistakes that the visiting side from Gardens were making. They were chiefly upset about the set pieces where they felt that the ball was not being put in correctly.

On one occasion as the visiting scrumhalf put the ball in, it appeared to rebound into his hands directly off the prop forward's leg. The referee allowed play to continue but suddenly a plaintive voice from the crowd was heard, "Ag, please Mr. Ref, how about l.b.w. then?"

⊕⊕⊕⊕⊕

The team discussion was taking place in the dressing room before an important game at Brandfort in the Free State. How were they going to stop the big threat, Domkrag, the visiting team's frontranker from Winburg, from his bullocking charges? After many ideas from everybody, ou Spyker the builder offered his bit from the corner.

"We must cannonize the bastard."

A hush fell over the dressing room, as many players had difficulty with the English language.

Young Grimbeek, a theology student home on leave, piped up, "Yes, we can use religion!"

"Ag, no, stupid, a blêrrie howitzer!"

⊕⊕⊕⊕⊕

During a match between De Aar (Railway Junction) and Prieska in the arid Northern Cape the two opposing props were 'having a go' from the first whistle, continuing hostilities throughout the game. Finally there was a lineout in front of the small stand. In the ensuing maul the Prieska prop clipped his opposition prop under the chin, knocking him over the touchline and for good measure, with a swagger, gave him a swift kick up the backside as he rolled into touch.

Oom Toppie, a loyal supporter, roared at the ref, "My bliksem, Mr. Ref, meneer, see that was not fair. He kicked him when he was in touch!"

🏉🏉🏉🏉🏉

It happened on the touchline farthest from the grandstand in the De Beers, Kimberley vs. Griekwastad game back in the '50s. Players were standing around the downed player as the referee was investigating the injury. Suddenly a player shouted to the line of spectators and officials on the other side of the field: "Plaster, please, plaster!"

A Red Cross man in uniform detached himself from the line and raced across the field with his first-aid kit. The player again shouted in despair, "Plaster, man, plaster!"

The flushed first-aid man, by now at full gallop bellowed back, "Damn it man, I cannot go any faster!"

🏉🏉🏉🏉🏉

A Springbok flanker, who had the nickname 'Tarzan', once had an altercation with the All Black prop, Knight. A flurry of punches was followed by a shrill blast on the whistle and both were asked to spend ten minutes in the cooler. Like two naughty schoolboys caught smoking they trooped off the field and squatted on the openside touchline.

A loud voice with a distinctive Cape flavour was heard above the roar, "Hey, Mr. Knight, you are blêrrie lucky it was not Jane that klapped you otherwise you would have been 'nights out'!"

🏉🏉🏉🏉🏉

A famous Springbok and Northern Transvaal flyhalf was on his way to practice at Loftus Versfeld. He stopped and picked up a hitchhiker in his shiny car. The passenger said that he was also going to Loftus.

After some distance the Springbok queried, "Are you coming to watch the practice?"

The passenger answered, "No, actually, I am going to the practice as well. But you won't know me ... I'm your inside centre."

🏉🏉🏉🏉🏉

Another famous Springbok and Northern Transvaal lock was going through a 'patch' in his play and his selection for the touring party was not a foregone conclusion. However, in the Currie Cup final against Western Province he had a blinder. He kicked a penalty, put over a monstrous drop from the touchline and ran in a great try. All the selectors and press were present at the after-match function.

At the reception a man from the press said to him, "Well, Frik, you had a great game, my man!"

He answered with a wry smile, "Ag, ja, man. Ek het geskop, gedrop en getry!"

The newspaperman concluded, "And gebok!"

Border, in their once-distinctive, chocolate-coloured jerseys were running riot against a hapless North Eastern Districts side in East London. With the score mounting, a rugby massacre was in the making.

An excited old salt from the Harbour Service bellowed out, "Dammit, Districts, there are brown streaks everywhere, even on your sterns!"

Talking about the Amatola region in the Border area of the Eastern Cape have you heard this one?

Van: "Hey, my boet, why are you walking so slowly?"

Piet: "I was kicked in the Amatolas playing against Pirates."

Van: "Yuslike! That must have been blêrrie painful, my swaer!"

A dejected Eastern Province supporter, who was getting used to the fact that his beloved Elephants were getting clobbered by all and sundry, wailed mournfully during a game at Port Elizabeth, "I think we should stop playing in the Currie Cup and try the Rice Paddy Cup!"

🏉🏉🏉🏉🏉

The famous Queenstown Swifts and Border twins were instrumental in demolishing the Amatola defence during a league match in Kingwilliamstown. After another blinding break by one of them an irate voice bleated forth, "My Gawd, Godley, that was not Godly, it was blêrrie Satanistic!"

DIE KEURDERS

OUR UNENDING ADMIRATION MUST be extended to those persons called selectors during the era of platteland rugby. Without them nothing would have been possible. Here is something to remember them by:

Dis saamtrek van verre
Ons kies weer ons sterre
Dis papier en kopkrap
En niemand gaan uitstap

After we've all let off steam
We'll have quite a team
We all have a say
To see who can play

Ons is almal vergader
So skuif almal nader
Kyk net na die uitslag
Van ons vorige slag

I say my Oom Klasie
There's no konsternasie
The result is no shame
It's only a game

Now, listen my boet
And feel my old foot
It's kicked a fine drop
Stop shaking your kop

Soos ek nou wou noem
He hulle ons goed mooi gedoom
Dit was ons heelagter
Ou Driesie die slagter

Now just a fine second
Remember who beckoned
Nee wag my ou Pellie
He slipped on his nellie

Now, okay my thirst
For we've chosen our first
What about the left wing
Nou hier kom 'n ding

Ou Manie's all right
Sometimes not so bright
But he has his day
That's all I'll say

Ons regtervleuel is wind
Hoe is jul gesind
A nod to inspire
He'll be a ball of fire

The centre, ou Venter
Is a real blêrrie slenter
Ek like die klein vaalkop
Wat ook dan kan skop

So, my maat in the middle
Is all of a riddle
He's always so go
For a helluva show

Nou sê ek vir julle
My manne en bulle
Die skakelpaar glans
Ek het julle sien dans

There is no other
With him and his brother
There's only one thing
They thinks they are king

Ag, please my ou Bokkie
Please press that old klokkie
The chief is so dors
Want ek het baie op die bors

Die damn ou potlood
Will ek gladnie meer stoot
Kyk net al die vanne
Van skikbare manne

Oom Koos dis so goed
Sit die name in hoed
Is jy dan spierlaf
Nou praat jy real kaf

It is now my round
And names to be found
Of two sturdy props
To give them the shocks

Ek like ou Piet Pompie
Has a fuse like a stompie
You're plenty dead right
In case of a fight

The other ou's name
Who's always so game
What about ou Blackie
With the broken takkie

My magtig, be careful
My beer is still near full
It's okay my brother
I'll get you another

My hooker is Farrell
He's round like a barrel
Now wait please you guys
This paper's small size

Oom Sakkie, the phone
And he lets out a moan
Dis weer die ou vrou
Wat will sy vra nou

Ja lieffie, my skattie
Ek het die rooi bakkie
Die enjin's nou puik
Nee, ek's gladnie skatryk

With his eyes to the sky
He lets out a sigh
Dis Dominee de Haas
Hy's hier op die plaas

Nee luister my liefie
Hier's gladnie meer rusie
Die span is halfway
En ons almal moet bly

Ja, ja, eks nou daar
Ons is amper al klaar
Ek is die hoofkeurder
Moet dink soos die speurder

Okay, my ou lam
By die Griek 'n nuwe kam
Ja, Kobus is hier
Hy sit by die vuur

Ta, ta, my engel
Nee gladnie meer hengel
Die klok staan op ses
Ons probeer ons bes

So, as I was saying
Why are you all praying
Julle's almal so stil
Nou, waar is ou Phil

Now listen my ou boet
How about that toot
Die tyd word so min
Ons moet weer begin

Nou praat ons van slotte
Nie hoenders en hokke
Ou Langbeen is maer
Maar hy's altyd net daar

Ja, ek weet hy kan spring
Dis altyd die ding
How about ou Fasie
To cause a sensasie

My magtig, my lewe
Dis amper half sewe
My life is at stake
I forgot the damn cake

Nee, gladnie een meer
Dis amper my keer
Well, if you insist
How can I resist

So, the slotte are fine
And what is the time
Now, onto the flankers
How about the two bankers

Ag, are they really so good
Or maybe we should
Try Hoender van Tonder
Hy try soos die donder

Nou luister my manne
Waar is al ons planne
Daars Bokkie le Roux
No, he's got the flu

Oh, after that tot
I nearly forgot
There's Bleskop Fourie
He's tall like a tree

There's skilpad van Wyk
He's tall like a rake
There's Blokkies Bruwer
The one that can swear

There's ou Krappies Koen
Wat alles kan doen
Please listen ou man
Let's complete the span

Nee, Pottie is reg
Dit was die geveg
As ons weer gaan verloor
Sal ons niks meer dan hoor

Die tyd is al sewe
My liewe ou lewe
Nee, hoe gaan jy aan
Ek's amper gedaan

Miskien te verspoed
Sit name in die hoed
Is julle dan mal
Dis 'n game met 'n bal

Ons het almal die stemreg
Wat ons hou en beveg
So put up your hands
As you make your stands

Allamagtig, van die vloer
Waar is my roer
It's a blêrrie split vote
Like I like to quote

Let's play Louis Luyt
At number eight
Now listen slim bloke
Until I have spoke

Casting vote I will cast
And that is my last
It's for Krappies Koen
Wat alles kan doen

Oom Sakkie, die foon
Hy is regtig beloon
Met die vroutjie so goed
En hy gryp sy hoed

Ag, luister, my kaatjie
Ek vat nou my baadtjie
Daars een plek nog oor
Vir die groot kokkedoor

Dis Dominee de Haas
Vanaf die plaas
Dis amper half tien
En die kos is bedien

Ag, dominee vergeet
Wat ons alles nou weet
U speel nommer agt
Op die Saterdag

MORE SIDESTEPS

TOMMY BEDFORD'S NATAL SIDE were getting the rough end of the stick against Northern Transvaal at Loftus when a boertjie yelled out, "The Last Outpost! Leave the out, out, and give us the Last Post!"

🏉🏉🏉🏉🏉

Overheard at a match between False Bay and Stellenbosch, "We don't need a new blêrrie backline. We need a new blêrrie railway line!"

🏉🏉🏉🏉🏉

A Waikato supporter lamented after the Springboks got hold of them during the tour match in Hamilton. "Halfbacks, three-quarters, first five-eights, second five-eights, for Gawd's sake just give us a whole player!"

🏉🏉🏉🏉🏉

Far North were really getting a pasting from Transvaal in Pietersburg when a spectator bawled out, "Far North, Far North, how far north must we go to get nought?"

THE NICKNAME PHENOMENA

THROUGHOUT THE THREAD OF South African rugby we find weird and wonderful nicknames. Some are descriptive and tell us about a person's build ... some about their strength and so on. Others have a special meaning known only to those parties involved during that period of their friendship. Listed below are some of those Springboks who were blessed with such titles. Also included are their provinces and the year they first received national colours:

Tiger Devendish	1891	Transvaal
Chubb Vigne	1891	Transvaal
Oupa Versfeld	1891	Western Province
Japie Louw	1891	Transvaal
Fairy Heatlie	1891	Western Province
Hasie Versfeld	1891	Western Province
Biddy Anderson	1896	Western Province
Scraps Wessels	1896	Western Province
Toski Smith	1896	Transvaal
Broekie van Broekhuizen	1896	Transvaal
Patats Cloete	1896	Western Province
Ferdy Aston	1896	Transvaal
Spanner Forbes	1896	Transvaal
Biddy Anderson	1896	Western Province
Japie Krige	1903	Western Province

Klondyke Raaff	1903	Griqualand West
Birdie Partridge	1903	Transvaal
Paddy Carolin	1903	Western Province
Oupa Reid	1903	Western Province
Rajah Martheze	1903	Griqualand West
Uncle Dobbin	1903	Griqualand West
P.O. Nel	1903	Transvaal
Artie Marsberg	1906	Griqualand West
Bingo Burger	1906	Border
Cocky Brooks	1906	Border
Sommie Morkel	1906	Transvaal
Boy de Villiers	1906	Western Province
Pinkie Daneel	1906	Western Province
Koei Brink	1906	Western Province
Mary Jackson	1906	Western Province
Cocky Hahn	1910	Transvaal
Koot Reyneke	1910	Western Province
Dickie Luyt	1910	Western Province
Boy Morkel	1910	Western Province
Boetie McHardy	1912	Orange Free State
Seppie Ledger	1912	Griqualand West
Baby Shum	1912	Transvaal
Saturday Knight	1912	Transvaal
Mannetjies Michau	1921	Western Province
Tokkie Scholtz	1921	Western Province
Royal Morkel	1921	Western Province
Attie van Heerden	1921	Transvaal

Tank van Rooyen	1921	Transvaal
Sas de Kock	1921	Western Province
Champion Myburgh	1924	Western Transvaal
Dauncie Devine	1924	Transvaal
Pally Truter	1924	Western Province
B.V. Vanderplank	1924	Natal
Sharky Osler	1928	Western Province
Espie van Wyk	1928	Western Province
Affie du Toit	1928	Western Province
Boy Louw	1928	Western Province
Boet Prinsloo	1928	Transvaal
J.C. van der Westhuizen	1928	Western Province
P.K. Morkel	1928	Western Province
Jock van Niekerk	1928	Western Province
Floors Venter	1931	Transvaal
Alvie van der Merwe	1931	Western Province
Ferdie Bergh	1931	S/Western Districts
Doc Craven	1931	Western Province
Ponie v/d Westhuizen	1931	Western Province
Fronnie Froneman	1933	Border
Lappies Hattingh	1933	Orange Freee State
Bunny Reid	1933	Border
Manie Geere	1933	Transvaal
Ginger Clark	1933	Transvaal
Ebbo Bastard	1937	Natal
Kalfie Martin	1937	Transvaal
C.B. Jennings	1937	Border
Flappie Lochner	1937	Eastern Province

Floors Duvenhage	1949	Griqualand West
Tjol Lategan	1949	Western Province
Buks Marais	1949	Boland
Kiewiet Brewis	1949	Northern Transvaal
Ballie Wahl	1949	Western Province
Hoppy van Jaarsveld	1949	Transvaal
Jorrie Jordaan	1949	Northern Transvaal
Outjie Geffin	1949	Transvaal
Fiks van der Merwe	1949	Northern Transvaal
Bubbles Koch	1949	Western Province
Ou Boet Strydom	1949	Northern Transvaal
Windhond Muller	1949	Transvaal
Fonnie du Toit	1949	Northern Transvaal
Salty du Randt	1949	Rhodesia
Carrots Geraghty	1949	Border
Cowboy Saunders	1949	Border
Basie van Wyk	1951	Transvaal
Jakkals Keevey	1951	Eastern Transvaal
Chum Osche	1951	Western Province
Jaap Bekker	1951	Northern Transvaal
Dolf Bekker	1953	Northern Transvaal
Natie Rens	1953	Transvaal
Bull Pickard	1953	Western Province
Sias Swart	1955	South West Africa
Vollies van Vollenhoven	1955	Northern Transvaal
Popeye Strydom	1955	Orange Free State
Butch Lochner	1955	Western Province
Basie Viviers	1956	Orange Free State

Peewee Howe	1956	Border
Mickey Gerber	1958	Eastern Province
Lofty Fourie	1958	South West Africa
Abie Malan	1958	Western Province
Mannetjies Gericke	1960	Transvaal
Spiere du Toit	1960	Boland
Lofty Nel	1960	Transvaal
Stompie van der Merwe	1960	Northern Transvaal
Mannetjies Roux	1960	Western Province
Attie Baard	1960	Western Province
Frik du Preez	1961	Northern Transvaal
Wang Wyness	1962	Western Province
Moff Myburgh	1962	Northern Transvaal
Trix Truter	1963	Natal
Haas Schoeman	1963	Western Province
Poens Prinsloo	1963	Northern Transvaal
Corra Dirksen	1963	Northern Transvaal
Tiny Naudé	1963	Western Province
Gawie Carelse	1965	Eastern Province
Snowy Suter	1965	Natal
Nelie Smith	1965	Orange Free State
Sakkie van Zyl	1965	Orange Free State
Albie de Waal	1967	Western Province
Tiny Neethling	1967	Western Province
H.O. de Villiers	1969	Western Province

Sakkie de Klerk	1970	Transvaal
Joggie Jansen	1970	Orange Free State
Piston van Wyk	1970	Northern Transvaal
Albie Bates	1970	Western Transvaal
Joggie Viljoen	1971	Griqualand West
Boland Coetzee	1974	Western Province
Gerrie Germishuis	1974	Orange Free State
Polla Fourie	1974	S/Eastern Districts
Moaner van Heerden	1974	Northern Transvaal
Klippies Kritzinger	1974	Transvaal
Kleintjie Grobler	1974	Orange Free State
Rampie Stander	1976	Orange Free State
Naas Botha	1980	Northern Transvaal
Gysie Pienaar	1980	Orange Free State
Okkie Oosthuizen	1981	Northern Transvaal
Hempies du Toit	1981	Western Province
Colin Beck	1981	Western Province
Vleis Visagie	1984	Orange Free State
Attie Strauss	1984	Western Province
Kulu Ferreira	1984	Western Province
Uli Schmidt	1986	Transvaal
Tarzan Small	1986	Western Province
Flippie van der Merwe	1986	Western Transvaal
Domkrag Erasmus	1986	Northern Transvaal

Faffa Knoetze	1989	Western Province
Lood Muller	1992	Natal
Grandpa Andrews	1992	Western Province
Balie Swart	1993	Transvaal
Naka Drotske	1993	Orange Free State
Japie Mulder	1994	Transvaal
Os du Randt	1994	Orange Free State
Toks van der Linde	1995	Western Province
Lem Honniball	1996	Natal
Vlok Celliers	1996	Western Province
Bullet Dalton	1996	Transvaal
Slappies Rossouw	1997	Western Province
Rassie Erasmus	1997	Orange Free State
Gaffie du Toit	1998	Griqualand West
Ollie le Roux	1998	Natal
Braam van Straaten	1999	Western Province
Butch James	2001	Natal
Bolla Conradie	2002	Western Province
Hottie Louw	2002	Western Province
Pedrie Wannenburg	2002	Northern Transvaal
Bakkies Botha	2002	Northern Transvaal

Other famous nicknames are: Baksteen Nel (Lions), Kapstok van Greunen (Transvaal), Griespomp Griessel (Griqualand West), Doppies la Grange (Lions), Cheese van Tonder (Transvaal), Kleinjan Tromp (Lions), Khaki Ferreira (Transvaal), Spottie de Waal (Transvaal), Chick Henderson (Transvaal and Scotland). There are many more but I thought these are sufficient to give the readers some insight into the mystery of nicknames in South African rugby.

🌲🌲🌲🌲🌲

The great All Black lock, Colin Meads was known as 'Pinetree'. During the second test against the Springboks at Newlands during the 1960 tour he played a blinder and also scored a great try. The New Zealanders were triumphant. Gatiepie was not impressed and was heard to mutter, "Pinetree befok! Ons moet nou 'n baobab gebruik!"

A TOURING UNIVERSITY OF Cape Town side was busy dishing out a hiding to Rhodes University in Grahamstown many years back. The hapless Rhodes side had no answer to the Ikeys' onslaught and the homeside supporters were becoming highly agitated that no points had yet appeared on the board for their team.

A kick upfield by the Ikeys' flyhalf found the Rhodes fullback completely out of position as the ball bounced about, unclaimed in open space.

A wailing voice was heard from the purple and white section of the crowd, "Oh, for heaven's sakes, Rhodes, do something!"

The gurgle of a high-powered motorbike engine was heard revving up from the side of the stand. The next moment, in a roar of dust, a hunched rider skidded onto the field, scooped up the ball and disappeared across the field amidst howls of approval from the Rhodians.

The perpetrator was banned from The Great Field for the rest of the season with no leave to appeal.

... Thanks Doc Seiler, you liked that one!

🏉🏉🏉🏉🏉

Buks Marais, Springbok wing and kicker, was of the bizarre habit of knitting in his new boots, by pouring water into them. He was performing this ritual during a training session for Boland for the pending game against Western Province at Newlands when a trawlerman strolled across the field and muttered, "Hy dink hy kan op die fokken water loop!"

An ardent Western Province supporter, sitting in a tree across the fence and watching the game with a cup in his hands, and holding onto a branch for dear life, put in his tuppence-ha'penny's-worth. Each word was preceded by his favourite word not found in dictionaries in those days, "Loose head! Vastekop! Going blind! Kick ahead! Rucking! Wat a blêrrie lekka game is dit!"

$$🏉🏉🏉🏉🏉$$

Sitting close to his dad at his first rugby game, Johnny, with big eyes riveted onto a loose scrum, uttered, "Daddy, look at what those ugly men are doing to each other, and they don't seem to mind!"

$$🏉🏉🏉🏉🏉$$

I remember the game well. Pirates were playing against Kokstad in Umtata. I put the ball into the scrum, which erupted, with the Kokstad front row lifted and blood streaming from the loosehead prop's nose. I knew that our tighthead, Gibby, was up to his tricks again. The ref was behind me and did not see the 'untoward play'.

During the following set pieces I was expecting retaliation from the Kokstad boys at any moment. But nothing happened.

They got on with the game ... no swearing, no fists and no late tackles. I couldn't figure this lot out.

At the reception after the game we got our answer.

Gibby was standing next to me at the bar counter with a beer halfway to his lips when the opposition frontranker walked in through the large doors. He was wearing the habit of a Franciscan priest with sandals and a rope-belt around his brown-cloth apparel. Gibby looked up and, in a shocked whisper, muttered, "Oh, shit, I've been hitting a priest all afternoon!"

Father Eric sidled up to him, turned his other cheek and pointed towards it, "It's that my man, or drinks are on you."

Gibby was so overcome that he spilled his beer and dropped his change all over the floor. They became great friends and Father got a convert to the faith.

$$\maltese\maltese\maltese\maltese\maltese$$

In the old days the field at Stutterheim on the Border was also part of the town commonage and cattle could be grazed there for a small fee payable to the municipality. Old Selbornians of East London arrived in their all-white strip and noticed that the place was full of fresh cattle droppings. It was decided that no scrums would take place over the offending areas. A fair decision welcomed by all the players.

Anyway, the game commenced but the visiting players couldn't sidestep the turds as well as their opposition. A strange aroma drifted from the playing area towards the few spectators lining the field.

Old Boys broke clear and the slippery ball was passed down the backline and onto the wing, who was being angled towards the touchline. Lyall, the Old Boys touch judge got so excited that he forgot his duties and yelled for the ball, running alongside the field, dropping his flag in the process. He received the ball and on a blinding, curving run was about to ground the ball under the posts when he slipped on a fresh pile and landed face first in it.

The opposition was stunned then burst out laughing and then protested the try. Lyall apologized profusely, but the local ref would hear nothing of the sort and banned poor Lyall from continuing as touch judge and threatened to report the matter to the B.R.U., which he later did.

At the disciplinary hearing, however, no one had ever heard of a touch judge being brought to book. He was dismissed with a reprimand.

🏉🏉🏉🏉🏉

Hamiltons of East London were up against Alberts of King William's Town when a Hamilton player called Whitey was sent off on the far side of the King Rec grounds. He walked very slowly around the posts towards the sure ire of the locals on the grandstand. The ref must have forgotten about him because as an Alberts player was streaking for the open line along the touchline he was jumped on from behind and bundled into touch near the corner flag. The ref ordered a lineout! The stand erupted as the touch judge came running up, shouting to the ref. Whitey's revenge was short-lived for when the dust settled the ref awarded a try under the posts. Whitey was banned for the rest of the season and helped with the coaching.

⬥⬥⬥⬥⬥

Cradock Rovers had come down to Tarkastad for a pre-season friendly at the Tarka showgrounds. The after-game gathering took place at the Royal and was a festive affair as was expected. Anyway, late that night it started raining and the Tarks lock decided that enough was enough and headed for his clapped-out Volksie. He got in, switched on lights and hit the engine. After a while he noticed a face at his window and accelerated again. Still the face remained, grinning evily at him through the pouring rain. He gripped the steering wheel tighter and put his foot down again. The face was still there as he passed out from fright. He later heard that some blokes had lifted his Volksie onto a mound of earth with the wheels suspended in mid-air.

⬥⬥⬥⬥⬥

As we know the Barberton daisy was the badge of Northern Transvaal and now the present-day Blue Bulls. A Northern Transvaal XV had travelled to Nelspruit and dished out a rugby lesson to bottom-of-the-log Lowveld. After the game a dejected Barberton supporter lamented, "En hulle het ook ons blêrrie daisies gesteel!"

HAKA

WE HAVE ALL EXPERIENCED the All Blacks doing their famous 'Haka' before a match and you might like to know the English translation:

There is going to be a fight between us
May it mean death to you and life to us
We will fight on or until our side is
vanquished
So long as the daylight lasts
We are here to continue the battle
To be either killed or to be victorious

Nice friendly bunch of blokes, hey!

WAR STORIES

A STRONG FORWARD, C.F. (Christiaan) Beyers, later
a combat general in the Anglo-Boer War of 1899–
1902, played for Pretoria. He played for the Transvaal
provincial side from 1892 to 1895. After the war
he resumed his practice as an attorney and rose to
become Speaker of the Transvaal Parliament under
the Responsible Government. After the outbreak of
World War I in 1914 he resigned his post and General
Smuts accused him of treason. He became involved in
the rebellion and was drowned in 1914 while crossing
the Vaal River, pursued by government troops.

STOPPING THE WAR TO PLAY RUGBY

THE RAIDING COMMANDOS OF General Smuts and
General Maritz laid siege to the rich copper-mining
towns of Okiep and Concordia in Namaqualand
during the Anglo-Boer War of 1899–1902. It was a
tiresome affair for both sides, as the conflict seemed to
be grinding to a halt. The weather was hot and dry and
boredom was creeping into the ranks of the besieging

commandos. It took a strong disiplinarian like Maritz to hold things together. Some sort of a message reached him through the ranks that the British would like to play a game of rugby against them. He considered the matter carefully and replied in letter form:

The Honourable Major Edwards
Okiep

Dear Sir,

I wish to inform you that I have agreed to a rugby match, taking place between you and us. I, from my side, will agree to order a ceasefire tomorrow afternoon from 12 o'clock until sunset, the time and venue of the match to be arranged by you in consultation with Messrs. Roberts and van Rooyen who I am sending in to you.

I have the honour etc.
S.G. Maritz
Field General
Transvaal Scouting Corps
Concordia
April 28, 1902

As the 28th April fell on a Monday the game was scheduled for the Tuesday but never took place. The story goes that the ceasefire was called by both sides and preparations were underway to stage this classic encounter when a gunshot rang out and both sides dived back into their trenches. Both sides blamed each other for the violation of the ceasefire. To this day we still do not know who pulled the trigger. The peace agreement between Great Britian and the Transvaal and Orange Free State republics was signed at Pretoria at the end of that month.

DESERT, RAIN, ICE OR SNOW... WE PLAY

PRIME CONTESTS BETWEEN THE leading rugby-playing countries leading up to the forties were undoubtedly those between the Springboks and the All Blacks. Theo Pienaar's Springboks had shared the series in 1921 on New Zealand soil and Maurice Brownlie's tourists salvaged a drawn series in 1928 in South Africa. Flip Nel took his Springboks to the Land of the Long White Cloud and won a famous series in 1937. Fred Allen brought the New Zealanders back to South African soil in 1949 and were white-washed 4-0 in the series. Felix du Plessis captained them to victory in three tests and Basil Kenyon led the Boks in the last test.

Although there were no official tests played between these two heavyweights during the period 1937 to 1949, any proximity between South African soldiers and their New Zealand friends and opponents always seemed to spark some talk about rugby.

Dozens of bars in Alexandria, Cairo and elsewhere up north bore scarred testimony as both Bok and All Black supporters tried to assert authority over the other. Even the dangerous threats posed by the Desert Fox, General Rommel, and his hardbitten Afrika Korps did not soften attitudes when it came to rugby.

There is a story that a South African received a rugby ball in his Christmas hamper from home and could not wait to have it blown up so that he could taunt his New Zealand friends. One morning he stood outside a New Zealand tent, tossing the ball up and down and asking the troops inside if they knew what it was. He was promptly bowled over by three tacklers.

In many of the matches, the sides contested a mythical trophy known among the troops as 'The Book'. Each side believed that the other did not know the laws of the game, giving rise to the question, 'Who wrote The Book?'. After each contest it was recommended, with suitable smugness, that the losing side should be given a copy of 'The Book' to improve its play.

This jovial rivalry finally came to a head in Rome during 1944 after the South Africans, New Zealanders and other colonial divisions had pushed the Germans back and occupied territory previously held by the Nazis. A 'test match' was arranged between the South African 6th Armoured Division and the New Zealand 2nd Division.

A rather physical encounter ended up with the South Africans running out the winners by 8–3. But surely the most deeply emotional encounters were those that took place in the various PoW camps dotted around Germany and Poland.

At the Stalag IVb camp in Germany a tournament was arranged consisting of eight sides including South Africa, New Zealand, Australia, England, Wales, Ireland, Scotland and a side of mixed colonials. The Boks were led by Fiks van der Merwe and emerged the overall winners. Fiks received full Springbok colours in 1949 playing flank in the first test against Fred Allen's All Blacks at Newlands.

Another encounter between the old rivals took place at the PoW Camp at Thorn in Poland. Once again, to the vexation of the men in black the South Africans won the game. A stout, young Jewish frontranker by the name of Outjie Geffin kicked the Kiwis into submission as he would again in the series in South Africa some five years later. Even more remarkable is the fact that the South Africans again were able to turn out in the famous green and gold jerseys (made in the camp). It is also known that the tough PoWs played in their bare feet in the middle of the Polish winter. Their spirit of commitment to the game was evident in the series put together only a few years after peace was declared in 1945.

BACK TO WORK ON THE RAILWAYS

MAN, OU GRAHAM, THE funniest story I ever heard was the one about Blackie Swart who had returned from up north and got a job with the railways in De Aar as a stoker. He was a keen player and was a centre for the De Aar side. He was strong and tough but a bit slow thinking ... you know what I mean, hey!

He was chosen to play against Prieska in two weeks' time but had to complete a trip up the line to South West and back. On his return he was hauled up in front of the superintendent, who had lodged a complaint against him for being rude to a lady.

Now you know those 15F engines have a big furnace and he had to keep shovelling the coal for long periods of time. He needed a lot of water to keep him going. Anyway they were coming up to Prieska and he had a helse piss on board. He could not wait for the station and climbed down onto the lowest footplate, unbuttoning his fly and hanging onto the rail with his other hand. He was still busy shooting into the air when they came round the corner into Prieska and passed the railway houses where a lady was hanging out her washing on the line.

Now being a good railway wife she waved at the engine but did not see Blackie hanging onto the rail with his dinges hanging out until it was too late. Now Blackie could not wave back because if he let go the rail he would have had a bad accident, you see. So what did he do? I will tell you. He blêrrie well waved his dinges from side to side and shouted, "Hallo daar, mevrou!" She let out a scream and ran into her house. The complaint arrived on the super's desk some time later.

At the official hearing the suprintendent, who had grown up on the footplates, let him off lightly. He had to do the trip over and go and apologize in person to the lady. He missed the game the following week against Prieska and became known as 'Die Slinger' up and down the lines in Namaqualand and the Northern Cape.

A TOURING TEAM FROM the Free State were spending the night at the Royal in Maclear after playing the game on the field next to the river. On occasions various players got their boots wet retrieving the ball from the spruit. As we know, it was customary in the old days to put your shoes outside your bedroom door to be cleaned and to be returned in the morning.

Now after a hectic party and singsongs the late-stayers made their weary way back to the outside annexe rooms. They saw a bloke making his way up the long passage collecting all the shoes and boots left outside and putting them into a large bag.

Ou Dolfie shouted to him, "Haai, wag vir ons, hier is ons skoene ook!" as they all removed their shoes and gave them to the collector.

The next morning at breakfast no one had shoes on. The thief had harvested a fantastic haul. A trader had to get special permission from the local police to open his shop for business on a Sunday. The entire touring party was kitted out with soft, white tekkies. From then on the trip became known as 'Die Tekkietoer'.

A Wepener player broke his arm after a match against a touring Viljoenskroon side during the after-match celebrations at the local. He accepted a bet to ride a bicycle along the bar counter and fell off as he swerved to avoid his captain's glass.

A Koffiefontein player returned home very late one night after a game and bragged to his wife that he had killed the longest blêrrie rinkhals he had ever seen. Early the next morning the couple wandered out to bury the reptile and discovered that their hosepipe was in a thousand pieces.

🏉🏉🏉🏉🏉

The once-proud Kenhardt team from the barren region of the northwestern Cape had a very fast and small wing in the team. After every Kenhardt win he performed his favourite party trick. He would push a straw up his nose and empty a double tot of brandy by sucking it up through his nostril.

🏉🏉🏉🏉🏉

Ou Knapie could never get to grips with the intricacies of 'die rooi taal'. It was no different when the coach issued the following instructions in the dressing room before a match against a powerful touring Diggers side in Klerksdorp.

"We must try and play in their half of the field, okay! So when you are in trouble kick at will.'

A confused Knapie was heard to mutter, "And we must now also learn their fokken names!"

🏉🏉🏉🏉🏉

During the same game Knapie was floored and raked by a Diggers player and was left dazed with his head in his hands. The ref came running up blowing his whistle.

"Did you see who it was?" asked the man in charge.

"Nee, I blêrrie well didn't, but I got a note of his fôkken number."

𝔉𝔉𝔉𝔉𝔉

In the old days the Royal in Komga in the Border area was also the rugby club headquarters. A local member, who had a military background and was a crack shot, took a bet one night after a match against Fort Glamorgan Prisons that he would shoot a beer bottle off his opponent's head at fifty yards.

A hushed pub watched in awe as the two protagonists stepped out onto the lit street to undertake the challenge.

By divine intercession the local priest, Father McManus, who was taking a stroll down the street, immediately put a stop to the proceedings by disarming the shooter and confiscating the rifle.

He promptly ordered them back to the pub!

𝔉𝔉𝔉𝔉𝔉

A popular mayoress of an Eastern Cape city opened a rugby festival by kicking the ball from the centre spot. A sports reporter asked her how she enjoyed the occasion.

She replied in all innocence, "I really enjoyed that and in future I would like to kick all their balls off!"

$$\maltese\maltese\maltese\maltese\maltese$$

A player from Tarkastad, who believed in the supernatural, overstayed his visit at the Royal after a game. He suddenly realized how late it was, said goodbye to everyone and drove his bakkie home, along the farm road. It was full moon, with a rustle of wind in the willows, as he approached the last gate on the road. As he neared the gate it swung open on its own. He jammed on brakes and would not get out of the bakkie. The breeze stiffened somewhat and he started getting cold. He was not too far from the farmhouse and decided to walk home across the veld. He took off on tiptoes towards the light in the distance, glancing back at the still-open gate. He fell into his own dam with a splash and realized that the light he had seen in the distance was a reflection of the moon on the water.

$$\maltese\maltese\maltese\maltese\maltese$$

Two mates from Despatch lived in the same block of flats and arrived home late after a game in Port Elizabeth. The one knocked gently on the door of his flat but received no response from within. He knocked louder but got the same response ... silence. His buddy suggested that he hoist him up along the drainpipe from the second storey. Our hero concurred and set his sights on the bathroom window as he clambered onto his friend's shoulders. He gripped onto the ledge and pulled himself up and partly through the small window. He was hopelessly stuck and could not reach the half-open door to heave himself through the window. There was an ashtray on the cistern below him, which he threw against the door, hoping it would cause the door to swing back towards him. It crashed against the door and shattered onto the floor. His wife gave a startled cry and dashed for the phone to call the police. Our hero identified himself to his hysterical wife by calling out her name. She regained her composure and tortured him by slowly looking all over the flat, calling his name ever so gently. Eventually she opened the bathroom door, blew him a kiss, and slammed it shut.

🏉🏉🏉🏉🏉

A bunch of farmers from the Komga district decided to stand themselves to a treat by going Union Castle from East London to Port Elizabeth to watch the test against the All Blacks. It was an overnight voyage with a change of ships in P.E. so as to be back in Slum on Sunday morning.

On their way to the field they pulled in to a beachfront hotel. One thing led to another as it started to rain. They decided to rather listen to the game on the pub radio than go to the Boet Erasmus stadium. They swore a pact of secrecy not to tell their wives about their change of plans. They were very nearly late for the ship but deft driving by a taxi driver got them there just as the gangway was being hoisted.

As all good secrets happen to leak out, one of the wives got wind of the affair some months later. Secretly the wives conspired to teach their wayward husbands a lesson never to be forgotten. They let out that because their husbands had enjoyed the live game so much they had all clubbed together and bought tickets for their men for the following test at Ellis Park. The boys could not believe their luck! At a gathering before their so-called departure the wives revealed their bluff ... no tickets.

Wicked things ...women.

The block of flats in Umtata was designed in the shape of a U. The cental courtyard area was all grassed with a tap to the one side. This particular player arrived home from an after-match function and climbed into bed naked, as was his habit of sleeping. He had just dozed off when a commotion broke out on the pavement with a woman shouting and screaming at the top of her voice. His actions were spontaneous. He jumped out of bed, rushed to the bathroom, grabbed a towel, draped it about him and dashed towards the action. The towel hooked onto the tap just as all the lights in the various flats went on and people crowded the windows. He was unaware of his condition as 'it' slapped from side to side as he ran. He came to a startling stop, looked down, covered himself with his hands and dashed back at double-speed into his flat. Clapping and wolf-whistles echoed in his ears as he hit the pillow.

🏉🏉🏉🏉🏉

Ou Tollie, a centre from Viljoenskroon, was asked how he was going to stop his opposite number on the coming Saturday against Koppies. He sat quietly for a moment, then answered, "Ag, man, you see, I will put in a tackle early even if it's late."

LIFE AFTER THE GAME

TWO TOUGH CAPE FISHERMEN went to watch a game at the Goodwood sports ground early in the '50s. After shouting encouragement and dopping all afternoon in the sun they were ready for home. Hero number one told his friend that he was going to take a shortcut to Thornton station through the Woltemade cemetery, as it was getting dark. His friend scolded him for being mad ... there were definitely spooks around.

"Djy mag bang wees, ma' nie ek, waai nou!" was his reply as he disappeared unsteadily into the murk. Things were quiet and the large cypress trees cast eerie shadows across the graveyard. He sat down on a tombstone for a smoke but cursed as he discovered his matches were with his friend.

He arose and headed towards the railway line. It was now quite dark and he did not see a newly dug grave directly in his path. He stepped into mid-air, hit his head on the side of the grave and landed at the bottom with a resounding thud. He finally came to and decided that he would spend the night where he was because he could not get out. He was dozing off when another thud disturbed him.

He realized that he had company and whispered, "Het djy a light vir my!"

A startled cry followed as the person disappeared upwards and sideways out of the grave without touching sides.

An article appeared in a Cape newspaper a few days later:

Will the person who jumped from a standing start out of a grave last Saturday night in the Woltemade cemetery please come forward, as it is estimated that this feat could be a new world record. A reward could be in the offing!

There were no takers.

DIE BEDONDERDE SPRINGBOK

A Springbok stood at the Pearly Gate
Bedraggled, bruised and late
St. Peter asked his name and date
And what was on Earth his fate

"I wore the green and gold for many a year
And scrummed against the best
First the All Blacks, then Wallabies and Welsh
In mud and all the squelch

"Then came the Pommies, Scots and Frogs
St. Patrick's Irish stole our togs
We broke the Pumas' luck
And smashed against their ruck

"But more kept coming along
Canadians, Tongans and the Pacific block
I took them on when I was strong
If you can but turn back the clock

"But I have to confess a sin
It was I who klapped Zinzan
Who landed in the sin bin
Dit was die lekka kan!

"The Italians drank our beer
They were all blêrrie queer
But a good time I have had
Ag, swaer, I took the good with bad"

St. Peter nodded his head and smiled
He slid back the bolt and rang the bell
"Step inside, my son," said he beguiled
"You have had your share of Hell!"

BEFORE THE ADVENT OF television we sat glued to our radio sets and heard the roar of the crowds and the voices of some great commentators. If any of them are still around I am sure they would not take umbrage if I mentioned them by name. They painted vivid pictures for us with their sayings and descriptions of these great events. We felt that they were our vital links to the outside world. Here are some of them.

The incomparable Gerhard Viviers whose sayings were legend:

Daar's die vaste skrum in die middel van die veld. Die Bokke se voorry sak en Dawie de Villiers sit die bal in. Die Bokke haak die bal en dis in die hande van Piet Visagie! Hy trap vas! Dis die skepskop! Dis hoog,! Dis uitmuntend! Dis manjefiek! Dis uitstekend! MAAR DIS HOPELOOS MIS!

The cool Chick Henderson, Transvaal and Scottish international:

The ball is in the hands of Carel du Plessis who swerves beautifully to the inside and evades the desperate defence of the Kiwis. He is still going! Oh, this poetry in motion, sheer poetry in motion!

on a high up-and-under onto the fullback ...

There's the Garryowen! This could be dangerous! This could be dangerous!

and ...

There is no trust amongst hookers!

and ...

I hope that was nothing untoward!

Gerhard again:

on Jaco Reinach sidestepping his opponent and belting towards the tryline ...

Hier kom spoed! Hier is spoed! Hier is spoed! Hier is spoed! Hier is spoed! En hy druk hom, druk hom!

and against the French as the frontrankers erupted, swinging at each other ...

En daar swaai die appels! Swaai die appels! Hier kom 'n ding! Hier kom 'n ding!

on Northern Transvaal against the British Lions ...

En die Leeus swaai die bal, Sharpe vat vas, maar word uit die aarde geduik deur Mannetjies Roux wat hom neersit soos 'n sak mielies!

THE GREYLINGSTAD SAGA

MAN, YOU SEE THAT mountain over there. Well, you can see a very big S.R. made out of rocks. That all happened during the Boer War. The Scottish Rifles decided to build a fort up there to keep a eye open on the railway line and the station over there. The Tommies were pushing up from Natal all along the railway line from Volksrust and Standerton. We blew up the small bridge near Val station and took a lot of food and ammunition from them. They were also easy to see coming down S.R. and we roamed around a lot, visiting our farms and families.

Anyway after the war we all returned to find many houses burnt and our sheep and cattle gone. We had to start again when we were with our families. Ja, let's go to the Royal and I will tell you more. Dankie man, I will have a brandy and water. Man, I think the trouble started in about 1909. You see, what started it all was the people from Willemsdal there up on the hill. The church had been built there and also a small school. The pastorie was also there and also the houses of the school head and one teacher.

Down here next to the railway line we had the post office and the store of Charlie Mannandale from Scotland. He fought for us so we all supported him, you follow. There was talk of the Standard Bank opening up here. As you can see it is here now. Somebody also was speaking about a mill next to the railway line. As you can see it is here now. The Transvaal Railways said that they would build station houses. As you can see they is here now. The second one from here is where I stay. I have only a few years to go on pension and will go to Heidelberg to retire where my son is with the Railways.

We had all heard about the Springboks in England under Paul Roos and decided to play rugby. The first problem was that we did not have a field, but at the small school was a level piece of ground. It was in Willemsdal, close by the church. A big thing happened now.

Ou Petrus Greyling sold a portion of his farm to the Transvaal government for a township, which they decided to call Greylingstad in his honour. The people of Willemsdal opposed the name. They said it should be named after Willem Bezuidenhout and called Willemsdal after his farm. His house was on the other side of the mountain.

Ag, man, for the first time the community was split down the middle. Up on the mountain we had the church, the school, the police station and another store on the road to Devon. The magistrate still lived in Balfour. Down here we had the railway, the store, a small mill, the bank and our market-place down the road towards the spruit. Oh, yes! and Tollie the blacksmith had just opened up. He was not so keen on church matters but fixed the dominee's buggy for free.

Meanwhile along the road at McHattiesburg the government changed the name of this place to Balfour because of the British prime minister. I tell you, my swaer, it did not help us at all. We were against the

English and liked the Scottish. They took away a Scottish name. Ou Mannandale nearly was sick for a month. I lie not to you. He used to give us credit as well.

Where was I? Oh yes, so Balfour was Balfour, but what were we? Greylingstad or Willemsdal? There were meetings in the small church hall and down here in the hotel lounge over there. The police station was moved down the hill and put next to the post office. As you say, things were getting hot in this area. Do not get me wrong, but I think the dominee and the skoolhoof were losing control up there. And we still had not had a game of rugby here. Balfour had played against Heidelberg and it was okay up until half-time. Never mind the rest!

The Transvaal government had heard about the dispute in our area and sent down three people by train to see what could be done. I was stationmaster at the time and welcomed them. Charlie had the first car here ... T.A.S. 1 was his number plate and he took them to meet the people from Willemsdal. He then left them for three hours and picked them up again. They stayed at the Royal and Hymie put on a dinner like you can't see! They went back to Pretoria and the name was to be Greylingstad on the map.

The rains fell all over the place before December and the mielies grew and the mill worked overtime. We were busy sending mieliemeel and everybody was happy.

The people of Willemsdal took it as a good sign for the decision and came down to do business in our area. The church opened an account with the bank and Tollie started to charge the church for repairs to its buggy and new car. Dingaan's Day was celebrated with Nagmaal at Willemsdal and a dance was held at the Royal Hotel for those who wanted. We accepted the voice of the dominee who said that at midnight no more piano music or dancing or drinking was to be done.

We had another meeting about our rugby club and I was elected as the president. I could not play well because of a Tommie bullet that went through my leg. Helena backed me all the way and said it was good for men and boys to do exercises in games. I had a helse problem about jerseys and colours. There were so many ideas that I had too many drinks that night. There were twenty men at the meeting and the Vierkleur was stretched out over the table. Charlie said that the flag of Scotland was blue and white and Kosie stated that white was good for all.

Nobody had even thought how we would get the jerseys. Everybody was getting up and down and going to the bar where other meetings were taking place. Charlie took charge and yelled for everybody to come back and listen to him. He had an idea ... a blêrrie good one! Now listen to this. He was a smous but a lekka oke. You know what I mean, hey?

He explained that the colour of green was for the mielies and the veld after the rains and it was also the main colour in the Vierkleur along the pole that held it up!

We now had over thirty people at that meeting. He also said that the colour blue was from the beautiful sky above them and was also to be found in the flag of Scotland. The meeting went mad and everybody started chanting about green and blue.

We had our colours now and Charlie promised to get us our jerseys. They arrived two months later in the summer.

Kosie Jooste at Greylingstad, 1933, in his Wanderers jersey. He had played for Transvaal U.19 a few years earlier.

We played our first game against Balfour in Balfour at the showgrounds near the cemetery. I think it was in 1910 after Union had been formed, because we all sang about 'Oranje, Blanje, Blou!', which were the colours in South Africa's new flag. We forgot about the Union Jack.

We went up in my train and came back in dribs and drabs as best we could on the Sunday. We had a dance at the Municipality and ou Kosie, our scrumhalf, kept our flag flying by waltzing onto the floor with a duck he had taken from some hok nearby. Even the concertina man stopped playing to have a good look at his steps!

The elders on the hill at Willemsdal had heard all about the dance and the dominee preached for the next six months about the evils of drink and temptations of the flesh. We kept our heads low and said nothing to anybody.

But do you know what? We won our first blêrrie game by one point. Frikkie kicked the penalty over the dwarslat but it should have gone higher but his toe took a sloot out of the ground just before the ball. He also got a loan from the bank and bought a tractor. I had to make a speech but forgot what I should have said. I could not get a loan because I was a government servant in the Railways.

We were by now becoming very fit because we ran up to S.R. and back to the hotel every Friday afternoon for practice. Happies once fell into Dokterskuilspruit on the way down, but that is another story. My railway was becoming very important because more and more trains was coming through to Durban. I got permission from Pretoria for Elsie to sell coffee and vetkoek to the passengers when the train stopped for water. I got promotion from a Grade D station to Grade C.

Pretoria sent five pounds down and asked me to make a garden next to the signal room.

We once went down by goods train to play against a railway side from Standerton. We were short of two players but stopped at Holmdene and picked up a tapper and his assistant. We won the game but they claimed that Holmdene was in their area and that we were poaching players. They got blêrrie upset when we beat them at arm-wrestling as well. Only half the team got to the dance that night. We all piled into the guards van of the mielie train late at night and woke up in Greylingstad on the Sunday. The train could not go any farther because of a law, which said that trading goods could not be carried on a Sunday. Some outjies slept until the sun was high, then went home.

I was then reported to Pretoria for turning a goods train into a passenger train and that nobody paid for the trip. I was let off with a severe warning and demoted to ticket clerk. My pay was chopped, but I could still live in my railway house over there. Elsie said not to worry because she would put up the price of coffee and vetkoeks at the station café. And I still had to look after the garden!

The stationmaster at Heidelberg, who I knew from the railway-training depot in Germiston, sent me a letter with the train and asked me to bring up a team in two months' time in June. I wrote back and said it was alright with us. He wrote back and said I must not come up by train with my team because then he would also be in the kak! Frikkie Bezuidenhout from Willemsdal phoned Pretoria and said he would pay for us on the goods train there and back. As ticket clerk I made out the receipt in duplicate and gave one to

146

Vossie when we got to Heidelberg. Frikkie went up by car to cheer us on.

I gave a pep talk to the men under the tin shed and pointed out that a member of Willemsdal had paid for our trip and that we were one in union now. We were a combined side from Greylingstad and Willemsdal. Everybody was 'hoor, hoor!' and we fokked them up 'big time' as the Englishman says. Corneels and Kosie could not come back with us because one had a broken nose and the other had a broken arm. They went to the hospital in Heidelberg and came back ten days later. Corneels later married his nurse!

The men were now so proud of the rugby team that they were wearing their jerseys during the week. I started a fund for more jerseys and we opened a savings account at the bank. I think by now we had played against Balfour, Standerton and Heidelberg and beat them all in a year and a half. We had a few more games and then as you know the war broke out in 1939. Half of the team supported Smuts and the other half Hertzog. I was a Smuts man because I was a government official, you understand? They paid my salary and gave me a house. Most of the farmers were all for Hertzog. Our rugby stopped because everybody was eyeing each other with suspicion. The club was 'kaput' as the Germans say.

My station was very busy with troops passing through to Durban so that they could sail up the coast with Smuts to fight the Italians and Germans in East Africa. Elsie sold a lot of vetkoek and coffee at the railway shop to the troops on the train. I was promoted back to stationmaster because Gert had to take over the station at Elandsfontein. And I still had to blêrrie look after the station garden as well.

After the war the place was not the same again. Everybody just wanted to be with themselves, you understand? Blêrrie politics took over again. It was now Smuts, Botha and Hertzog all mixed up with each other. Some wanted English spoken, others just wanted Afrikaans in the schools. The road to Balfour was graded and more cars were being bought. The outjies were going to Balfour more often by road and so it was the end of our rugby club. It was sad, very sad. I retired to Heidelberg in the end.

THE PENGUINS OF
LÜDERITZBUCHT

A firm handshake greeted me with "Aangename kennis" from behind his shop counter. The little fishing village was surrounded by rocks and sand and overlooked the harbour where fishing boats were snugly riding at anchor. The weather had abated a bit and the shop was clear of sand on the floor.

Lüderitz harbour in the old days. Supplier of rugby players for the Penguins.

JA, MAN, WE USED to play rugby here. Down by that field just out of town on the road to Diaz Point. Ja-nee, you are right, the one with no grass on it by the saltpan, surrounded by stones to mark the area. Sometimes the salt came up and we were not sure of the chalk markings on the ground to tell us where in the field we were, you understand. Sometimes the ref had to blow for a break to get the sand out of our eyes. One oke nearly died because of a smother tackle in the sand.

Lüderitz rugby field.

Ja, man, we used to play in the Ring Section South. That was Lüderitz, Bethanie, Keetmanshoop and sometimes Aus, if all the police were available from that station. The mine at Rosh Pinah had some grass on their field and were included in the Ring. It was nice to play there because sometimes we could sleep over in the rooms of miners on leave and the beer was very, very cheap. They also had good music from a jukebox with flashing lights. Some of the boytjies invented dancing steps to this music that twisted their knees and ankles, you see.

One weekend we had to go to Bethanie to play. All we had for transport was two bakkies. We all piled onto them outside of Kapps Hotel in the morning. We were near Kolmanskop when Freek shouted that he had left his togs in the bar. We turned back and the other bakkie said it would go slow for us to catch up. We found it just otherside of Haalenberg station with a flat tyre and no spare one. The wind was starting to blow and sand was coming over the road in heaps.

It was decided to leave Herman's bakkie on the side of the road with a note inside that we were coming back at a later time. Us fifteen okes, plus two officials, got onto the other bakkie and headed for Bethanie, only some hundred miles away. The wind was stronger and we were all standing up together gripping each other for support. The blêrrie middelmannetjie was high sometimes and we sommer sailed over it scraping the bottom of the bakkie. Two cars passed going to Lüderitz and they waved and blew their hooters. They thought it was funny. Blêrrie funny! Our legs were cramping and we had to stop sometimes for a leak, you know.

Behind us some bloke started hooting through the dust and we all turned around at the same time and nearly all fell over the side together. Oom Vlekkie passed us and stopped some way ahead. We crawled up to him in the skemerlig and listened to what he had to say. He told us that he had seen the deserted bakkie near Haalenberg and decided to come to our rescue at once.

We all shouted thanks, and half of us jumped onto his bakkie as others threw their small suitcases in as well. We were already late for the game but the Lüderitz boys were on their way again, plus a new supporter.

We arrived all tired and bedonderd at the hotel in Bethanie and was busy ordering beers when one of the officials told us to get to the field as the game was going to be played. It would start at 8 o'clock that night! It was now 7 o'clock. Some boys changed their orders to Klippies and Coke and the hotel owner was very upset because he had already opened a dozen or so beers and now had to find the tops and put them back on again.

We told him we would be back after the game to sort things out. He was still all suurbek and Gansie told him to piss off or something like that.

The word had got around that we were in town and would be playing after all the gedoente of getting here. We decided to change at the field and all trooped out in single file and climbed onto the transport cars again.

An amazing sight greeted us. There was the field surrounded by all the cars in the district with their lights on. I think that that was the first floodlight game in South West Africa ever! Most of us changed into our rugby togs around the bakkies. Our yellow jerseys showed up well in the lights as we ran onto the field with only a few hooters blowing for us. Bethanie followed us and every blêrrie hooter in the district went off in our ears.

The game was on! I was playing lock and slipped in

a scrum and banged my nose on a boot and it started bleeding. The ref thought that I had been punched and gave us a penalty. Gatties lined it up and moered it straight through the middle. Two hooters blew. Lüderitz 3, Bethanie 0. We were getting tired and decided that up-and-unders would help us. The high kicks were lost in the heavens and both teams stood around waiting for the blêrrie ball to come down from the darkness. As it hit the ground we were blinded by the car lights and grabbed at anything moving! I grabbed a collar without the ball and the ref saw it. Penalty. Lüderitz 3, Bethanie 3. Forty car hooters blew!

Our try was, as the writers would say, 'a gem'. It happened like this. We were only five yards from their line for a set scrum. Just before we crashed into each other Miguel, our hooker, coughed into the face of the other hooker who moved his head sideways and we pushed them off the ball straight away. The ball went to our first centre who was a relative of our hooker through marriage.

He caught the ball but at the same time got a cramp in his left leg and doubled over in pain. His opposite number went diving into mid-air with his tackle and Mannie fell over the line under their posts in agony. Gatties was on the target. Lüderitz 8, Bethanie 3. The half-time whistle blew. Some okes just sat down where they were standing.

The ladies of Bethanie came onto the field and we all got our half-slices of oranges. The two big water buckets on the halfway line were also emptied as some blokes poured a mug of water over their heads to wash the sand away.

Mannie was buggered and could not get onto the field for the second half. We were down to fourteen men. At half-time I told the men that there was only one ball that we were playing with. I pointed to a very big thorn bush on the side of the field between the halfway line and twenty-five. We had to kick the ball into that bush so as to get some rest during the second half when needed. Gatties did a fine job and we rested a lot.

We decided to stick to eight forwards and play that way. The wing position was dangerous because he was always close to the line of rocks following the touchlines on the sides, you understand? Anyway, they started to run at us in a big way. We tried up-and-unders again but the ball always bounced to them. They did the same to us and Bles, our fullback, got a broken nose when a high ball from the dark heavens landed on his upturned nose. They picked it up and scored next to the right-hand upright. We tried to charge the conversion down but the scores were level. Lüderitz 8, Bethanie 8. The car hooters blew long and loud and so did the referee's police whistle. The game was over at last. We hung over the sides of our bakkies and some blokes coughed a lot.

It was now half past nine at night as we all went to the hotel for a shower or a bath. Some blokes went straight into the bar and stayed like that until we left. I was getting worried about the trip back home and phoned the hotel at Goageb and asked for my pal who was the owner. I ordered two cases of beer and asked him to have them ready when we passed through as we could be in a hurry. He said okay!

I was feeling relaxed and contented that we had played well and the party mood was starting to gryp. I looked at the bar clock again and it had gone to half past ten. South African laws said that all bars must close at 11. p.m., you remember? I sounded the alarm and we piled onto our bakkies and raced towards Goageb to be on time for our beer.

We pulled up in front of the hotel and I ran into the entrance after eleven to collect our order. My pal Frans was waiting for me and asked the score. I told him and he said that the beers were on the house. That is another story. When I got outside there was the train to Lüderitz taking water and blowing the boilers at the station. The ticket office was closed but all the younger outjies wanted to go back to Lüderitz by train. With beers in hand they tried to bribe the conductor who had the green flag. He was new on the rail and was uncertain what to do. The engine driver kept blowing his whistle asking for the green flag. One of the blokes pinned his arms to his sides so that he could not raise his flag. I went up to the engine driver, who was a pal of mine, and told him the story. He said that he had seen nothing but he knew that the open truck in front of the guardsvan was empty. I said thanks. They let go the guard and jumped into the truck. I waved the green flag towards Ben. He opened the valves, let go the brakes and half our team was safely on the way home. The guard later started telling jokes across the connecting rods between the trucks.

Klappies, our bakkie driver, decided to beat the

train back to Lüderitz. He took that right turn onto the main road with a sharp turn and two suitcases went flying into the dust. We banged on the roof and told him he was mad and out of his blêrrie kop because he was going too fast. He stopped very quietly and waited until we had got the suitcases back. He then drove very slowly and we were getting cold on the back. Our beer was getting low and we wanted home, you understand. The more we asked him to step up the speed the slower he went. He was a total fokop that night. He had the mind of a blêrrie welder and that was all.

Our other bakkie had left us behind and would get to Lüderitz before sun-up, for sure! The train was now on our left side and we kept on asking Klappies to go faster. He shouted that he wanted to make sure it got to Lüderitz on time. It passes Guibes because there was nothing to pick up, but had to stop at Aus to pick up a policeman who was transferred to Lüderitz. Klappies kept to the road and we saw the train again near Garub. By this time two blokes were talking to themselves curled up in their rugby jerseys. The one said something about using his Luger on a Sunday. The lights from the train flicked across the sand again and we knew we were not alone in the world. Then they disappeared again around a bend. It said goodbye on the whistle.

At Tsaukaib we were still level with each other but a clattering of teeth was heard from the bottom of the bakkie. One oke put a suitcase on top of him to keep out the cold and recited the 'Onse Vader wat in die Hemel is'. My feet were now not belonging to me and I loosened my tog laces and shook out the dust from my togs. By mistake I sat on the suitcase and the body below it heaved upright and I hit my head on the side of the bakkie. There was a lump. Two okes were now staring at each other but could not speak. It was the coldest night recorded since the turn of the century. I had once read a book about sailors on a raft in the cold Atlantic clapping hands and singing to keep awake or die from the cold. We did just that now. Klappies was nodding his head in tune to our rhythm and tapping his fingers on the steering wheel. The blêrrie fool thought that we were enjoying ourselves. He was still travelling at 20 m.p.h.

The old Grazplatz station on the Lüderitz–Keetmanshoop line.

Haalenberg, and we were still level with the train.

Time about 5 o'clock in the morning. Rotkuppe, Grasplatz and Kolmanskop in sight. The beautiful black rocks and the cemetery were in sight. The sun was coming up and then Klappies put his foot on the accelerator and we roared down the main street, crossed the railway line and stopped outside the station. The train chugged in a few minutes later and slowly came to a stop. We were all safe and sound as the Englishman says. It was Sunday morning at 7 o'clock. The Catholic church was ringing its bell for service and Seekat the beggar was starting his rounds.

We could not get Hans off the bakkie because he was too stiff to move. His one leg was straight in front of him and his eyes were staring like into nothing. Fanus was still gripping his suitcase handle but his hand was locked around it. He slowly lifted his head, smiled and went into a trance. Sampie thought that he was okay, slided off the rear end but fell into the sand and could not move at all. I walked like a man on stilts and stood in the cold sunlight looking at this lot. Klappies was still grinning and asked us if we liked his driving and was the speed okay. We were too forlorn to murder him on government property. Somebody grunted that he was going to fill in a 'Injured on Duty' form and hand it in to the committee.

Jannie Klooser smiled as he concluded his epic story about his greatest game for the Penguins of the Angra Pequena Rugby Club, Lüderitz, South West Africa. He ended his story by telling me that some bloke had torn his Penguin badge off his shirt while they had been playing and never noticed it until his jersey came out of the wash the following Monday.

THE TROJANS OF TARKASTAD

TARKASTAD, WHERE THE HELL is Tarkastad? This I have heard on many occasions. I reply that they should have listened to their Geography teachers at school. Some of the replies to that cannot be printed. Well, if you must know, it is halfway between Queenstown and Cradock and still has a Royal Hotel to boot. The rugby field is still at the showgrounds and they still have games there, sometimes. The last time that I was there the post that was near the road to the Winterberg was at an angle that is definitely not acceptable in terms of South African rugby legislation.

🏉🏉🏉🏉🏉

This tough, dry sheep-farming area spawned many young boys who were packed off to boarding schools such as Queen's College in Queenstown, Dale College in King William's Town and St. Andrew's College in Grahamstown, to mention but a few great rugby-playing schools. They came back to farm after leaving school and many signed up during the Second World War into the famous D.M.R. (Die Middelandse Regiment) to fight against Rommel in the North African desert. The small Anglican and Presbyterian churches bear the rolls of honour to the fallen sons of this area.

Early Scottish settlers had nudged their way up the wild Baviaans River leading into the cold Winterberg range of mountains bordering Tarkastad. They settled, survived and multiplied. It became the breadbasket for hundreds of surrounding miles in the mid-1800s. Names like Cameron's Glen, Glen Lynden, Glenthorn, Thomas Pringle's Cabin and Newstead, are still to be found.

A young soldier named Ken returned from up north and invested in a farm on the banks of the Tarka River, which was normally dry in winter. The restless spirit of these young men who had seen action and death was enhanced and tamed by the game of rugby. Ken told me that all he wanted to do was practise and play rugby. His father, who had previously captained Tarkastad, understood his boy's emotions but with suggestive persuasion also brought farming into the daily routine. Dams to be built, windmills to be erected, gates, fencing and a hundred and one other things that were necessary to build a farm from a government grant issued to ex-servicemen.

Across the sea in New Zealand young men were in a similar position rebuilding their lives or starting them anew. They were rugby men, like Ken, and remembered the losses they had suffered at the hands of the South African troops during various games in the desert and Italy. They were no doubt itching for revenge and the possibility of renewing friendships severed by the Allied victory. Also to their chagrin was the series win by the Springboks in New Zealand in 1937. The stage was being set for a monumental encounter between the two giants of world rugby.

Ken told me that his father captained the Tarkastad first team in 1924 and won the Border Grand

Challenge. This was no mean feat for a small farming community facing strong sides from East London and the Transkei. The green jerseys with white collars and cuffs were becoming known throughout the Eastern Cape and Border rugby areas. We sat on his verandah with coffee in hand and the sun warming his aching knees. With a broad smile and delightful Eastern Cape accent punctuated with isiXhosa expressions he warmed to the occasion.

꧁꧂꧁꧂꧁

Yes, Skip, I will tell you about it all! Before the war in 1939 I played on the flank for Tarkastad firsts and we won the Moodie Cup, which was played by teams in our Swifts region. We beat Pirates, Villagers, Dordrecht and I think Cathcart. I'm not so sure anymore. Anyway, war broke out and there was a recruiting meeting by the Defence Force in Tarkastad at the magistrate's court. I went and listened and immediately signed up with a lot of other blokes. I would have liked to join the First City Regiment from Queenstown but we fell under the Karoo region. I was captured by Rommel at Tobruk and was 'in the bag' for three years.

I came back home in 1945 and started playing rugby again. I was quite fit and was selected for Swifts of Queenstown in 1946. I nearly fell off my chair when I was selected for Border in 1946 to play against Natal in Durban. We went up in three cars and two cars filled with supporters followed us through the Transkei to Durban. The last time I was there was boarding a transport ship in the army. On coming back from Natal I was fortunate enough to be chosen for Swifts again and I captained them during 1947 and 1948. I also captained Tarkastad during this period and we won a new trophy called the Tiffin Cup. In 1948, I was a member of the Border team and we played against Griquas, Transvaal and North Eastern Cape. We went by train. After having a few beers with the Transvaal boys at Ellis Park I heard that the All Blacks could be coming over in the next year.

I was back on the new farm but could not seem to settle down. My dad was sympathetic and left me alone. I went to practice and ran along the farm roads as an extra keep-fit session. I had worn the famous chocolate jersey of the Border and I felt good about it. The *Daily Dispatch* of East London confirmed that the All Blacks were coming and that their first match would be against Border in East London. Date set 15th June 1949. My heart stopped, Skip. I could not think straight. Youwww!

The All Blacks had arrived in South Africa by ship while I was busy with a fence leading up onto the mountain behind the small farmhouse we lived in. I cannot remember the date but our nommer-assemblief man at the Tarks exchange rang our number and said there was somebody from Queenstown on the line.

"Hullo, Ken. Congratulations, you are in the Border side to play the All Blacks in East London in two weeks' time. Do you accept? If not, tell me now, because we will have to find a replacement.

"Oh, and by the way, if you accept, you will have to find your own way to East London. The Border team is booked in at the Strand Hotel in Oxford Street."

I said a weak, "I accept" and sat down quietly, still dazed by it all. The Swifts Rugby Union congratulated me and the farm lines were jammed with messages from all over the district after the team appeared in the *Daily Dispatch*. It read as follows:

The following players have have been selected to represent Border against Fred Allen's All Blacks at the B.R.U. on 15th June 1949:

C. Snyman	Old Selbornians
M. Saunders	Hamiltons
S. Geldenhuys	Cambridge
G. Johnstone	Old Selbornians
C. Geraghty	Hamiltons
J. van Rensburg	Buffaloes
G. Woodward	Buffaloes
H. Pretorius	Cambridge
P. MacKenzie	Cambridge
E. Smith	Cambridge
S. Raath	Buffaloes
R. Brock	Old Selbornians
R. Gordon	Cambridge
K. King	Swifts
B. Kenyon	Transkei (captain)

The only players from outlying areas were Ken King and Basil Kenyon (who would later captain the Springboks). The rest of the team were all from East London.

Tarka Rugby Football Club, 1948. Winners of the Tiffin Cup. Back row: R. Erasmus, K. Scott, D. McEwan, E. Webster, N. Levey. Second row: E. Hunt (Selector), P. Budler, N. Barnard, T. King, V. Cockin, H. van Vuuren, B. du Plessis (Rep. Swifts Selec. Comm.) Sitting: K. King, A. Bryant (Captain), S. McEwan (President), J. King (Vice-captain), M. Botha. Front row: E. McEwan, T. Herselman

Ken got on the overnight milk train to Queenstown from Tarkastad and caught the mainline train to East London the following day. He walked from the station to the hotel only to discover that he had not been booked in and the hotel was full up with supporters from all over the Border region. No problem, he slept on the floor in a bathroom. Basil was staying with family and the rest of the boys were at their homes in town

The following day he caught a taxi to the grounds and was greeted joyfully by his Border teammates on arrival. The rest is rugby history. Border tackled with fire and rattled the All Blacks completely. The centres forced the feared New Zealand backline to cut inside, only to be snuffed out by the loose forwards, Kenyon, King and Raath. Kenyon swooped on a loose ball and dived over for a try. 'Dagga' Snyman slotted two penalties and the end whistle blew. The crowd went beserk with joy and the All Blacks formed a line and clapped the local lads off the field.

It was a stunning victory by any standards and the All Blacks were magnanimous in defeat and made many friends. Ken was still sitting in his togs waiting for a shower when in walked Crowley, his opposite number, with a cold beer in his hand.

He gave it to Ken and said, "See you later cobber. You owe me one!" Great stuff in those days. It must be remembered that back up north during the war some of the players from both sides had actually met each other during rugby games in the PoW camps and elsewhere.

Ken also mentioned that during a game between them in the PoW camp in Germany, a German guard rushed at them blowing his whistle and calling for a back-up platoon. Because they were tackling each other he thought that a fight or a riot had broken out. With smiles they made him understand that they were playing a game. He rolled his eyes and muttered,

"Mein Gott! Der Englander ..." and tapped his head with his finger to indicate madness.

More madness was to follow when the All Blacks played Border again in East London in a match before the fourth test at Crusader Park in Port Elizabeth. The 17th September 1949 was another highlight in the annals of Border rugby. The All Blacks were thirsting for revenge and named a near-test side to do battle. Thirteen players who were to be selected for the following test against the Springboks were included in the side. Border made one change through injury. M. Botha of Swifts of Queenstown was in for the Old Selbornian, Brock. Ken had a travelling companion from his area. They were both booked into a hotel this time around.

Again, the Border tackling was up to standard and the heavier All Blacks were finding it difficult to cope with the speed of the defence, marshalled with brilliance by Basil Kenyon from the Transkei. Ken flew headlong into the hip of a forward and was dazed for a few minutes but refused to go off.

Johnny Simpson, the tough frontranker from Aukland was heard to mutter, "This is going to be a damn bloodbath!"

Geraghty, with his flaming red hair, was everywhere. Graham Johnstone, the centre, sent Peter Henderson, the Empire Games 100-yards champion, staggering into the fence with a try-saving tackle.

The crowd was chanting, "Bordah! Bordah! Bordah!" and the segregated community behind the posts were clamouring over the small fence to pat their heroes on the back. The South African Police had to persuade them to keep their seats. The score was 6–6 when the final whistle blew. Ken took a beer over to his opposite number Crowley in the All Blacks' dressing room. The Springbok side for the final test was announced and Basil Kenyon became the new captain. Also selected was Carrots Geraghty who had played a brilliant game on the wing. A small province, by South African rugby standards, had pulled off the unbelievable rugby miracle ... twice!

Rugby in the Border platteland got a new lease of life. Kenyon, King and Botha put their experience back into local rugby for many years afterwards. The chocolate-coloured rugby jersey legend had been born.

"Tarkastad, where the hell is Tarkastad?"

A lot more people knew where it was after that lot!

TARKASTAD AGAIN ... SORRY, HEY!

As RECENTLY AS 2004 A.D. another game was played at Van Riebeeck Park, alias The Showgrounds, on the edge of this semi-Karoo dorpie. To qualify you had to be over sixty years of age. Handwritten A4 posters were stuck onto the two shops' windows as well as the two bottle stores. The local chemist chipped in as well with full support. The one and only doctor said he was available. The taxidermist decided to start practising by doing two press-ups per day. The opening meeting took place at the Royal Hotel and a date was set. All proceeds were to go to the local hospital. All selected players had to pay to play.

"Outjies came out of the woodwork," explained Danie Kilian from Kili's Take Aways in the main street. His main business was supplying truckers passing through, with hissing brakes as they pulled up on their way to the hinterland and Cape Town via Cradock.

"You know, Graham, it was the easiest blêrrie job I have ever had! I had more players than I could use. I know of a few blokes who were under sixty, but what the hell! We needed money for our little hospital. We have to pay the staff."

At the organizing meeting everybody was welcome to say his bit. It was decided that the game should be a game of touch rugby. Everybody bellowed his approval. It was decided that some form of footwear should be worn. Everyone nodded in agreement. To distinguish the two sides from each other it was decided that one side should wear anything white and the other blue. All approved the motion without a problem. Somebody suggested that the wives should line up as pronkpoppies and cheer the men on. A roar of approval greeted this suggestion. Francine got the job to whip this section into shape. The referee was to be a man of integrity and impartiality and have a sound knowledge of the game. Johan, the bottle-store owner, got the job. He accepted gracefully after being met with clapping from the floor.

Before the game and injuries. Tarkastad showgrounds 2004.

The match was to be played in three weeks' time and the bar at the showgrounds was asked to deal with the anticipated extra orders ... to accommodate a looming thirst factor later that day. That was to be bakgat, no problem, fixed up! Some of the men had a problem convincing their wives that it was only a slow game with no tackling involved. There was no danger whatsoever regarding broken bones etc. Anyway Doc de Witt would be playing so as to warn the guys about ill-health breaking out on the field. Everything was under control, no problem, fixed up!

It was three o'clock on a warm Saturday afternoon when the two teams walked onto the field through the tunnel of pronkpoppies. The stand was full and a buzz of excitement rumbled amidst nervous laughter and apprehension. The doc took up his place for the kick-off close to his forwards but was promptly sent to fullback so as to be at hand if his skills in the medical field were required. No good having a damaged doctor on the field.

Pep talk.

A side-footed stab at the ball from the centre spot got the game underway. It went about three yards, but the ref shouted, "Play on!" Somebody had a fly-hack at the ball but missed. Somebody picked it up but was immediately touched by someone. It was touch rugby, so a scrum was ordered. The biggest man on the field was the taxidermist and he stood like a lone sentry waiting for his opposition to come closer ... to sak down. Everybody kept pushing everybody forward from the opposing sides into the squashed frontrank positions. He stood there grinning and beckoned them on with a gentle hand signal. The ref stepped in and warned him for robust play in advance.

Cheerleaders.

"I haven't done a blêrrie thing yet, Mr. Ref. Be a sport!"

A shrill blast on the whistle and he was called aside to receive a lecture of note. He called upon one of his teammates, the magistrate, for advice on legal affairs but was strongly advised to adhere to the law of the whistle. He went back to his mark, bent forward and waited silently for the scrum to form around him.

Hotting up.

"No pushing allowed!" bellowed the ref. The ball was rolled in gently and came dribbling out at the back of the scrum. An over-zealous flank could not resist the temptation and tackled the hapless scrumhalf.

A shrill blast of the whistle stopped proceedings, as the ref lunged into his trouser pocket for a red card. The two captains came rushing forward for a discussion and persuaded the ref that 'soft tackling' should be permitted. Agreed, everybody happy? Okay, play on! The game was now controlled by the players with gusto and zest.

The ref got back into the act by sending off Pieter Herselman for smelling in the scrum. He had previously been tackled and had fallen into a heap of cow dung. That was the first red card of the match. Another player simply ran onto the field and promptly took his place. The ref agreed.

Kili side-stepping and kicking ahead. The results, a displaced patella.

The story now becomes somewhat complicated because at half-time a certain cooling beverage was supplied to certain players to quench their thirst amidst the swirling Karoo dust. It is, however, a known fact that some players kicked their footwear off and decided to play kaalpoot. It is also a known fact that a total of four red cards flashed to send players to early cold showers. The three remaining red-card transgressions cannot be clearly remembered but would be brought up at the next meeting.

It is a known fact that Johan the ref forgot about the time and constantly blew his whistle when he could not keep up with the game. Furthermore, the score was certified by Kili but he was not sure which side had won the battle. Some side won 17–12. The final whistle eventualy blew and the doctor, magistrate, taxidermist, policemen, bank manager and his clerks, post-office officials, shopkeepers, bottle-store owner and farmers trooped off the field, cheered by the ladies festooned in blue and white. The English parson limped off, walking slightly bent.

As is customary after every battle, a casualty list appeared, nailed onto the door of the magistrate's office. However, in this instance the doctor was confronted with the following:

⇨ One oblique fracture of upper ulna in the right arm, because of undue pressure from a downward movement. (Somebody tackled him.)

⇨ One slightly abnormal sternum resulting in

a bent concave structure because of undue weight from heavy downward pressure being asserted upon this area. (Somebody sat on him.)

⇨ One slightly bruised kidney, mainly protected by the pelvis structure, but due to an unusual angle contact abrasions are evident. (He was tackled from behind, above the belt.)

⇨ Two damaged phalanges in the left hand with possible greenstick fractures, caused by downward pressure on abnormally positioned bones. (He fell forward with outstretched fingers.)

⇨ One indented lower rib, comprising number seven on the left-hand side, resulting in a division of tissue from the structure. (He fell on the rugby ball.)

⇨ One abnormally twisted right metatarsal on main toe with no destruction of tissue in evidence, coupled with a slight distortion of the number-two structure next to it. (He buggered up his toe when he kicked the ball without his takkies on.)

⇨ One slightly displaced patella resulting in slight movement to the outside of the right structure. (He tried to sidestep.)

⇨ One muscular-inclusive section binding the upper structure of the upper rear leg, comprising of muscle and tissue binding the pelvis in concordance. (He pulled a hamstring.)

The lame and late entered the clubhouse at the showgrounds after showering and patching up their wounds. The display of food put on by the women was, to say the least, fantastic. Tarkastad had certainly chipped in for their M.O.T.H.S. hospital. Ah! As you can see the game is alive and well in Tarka. They have started organizing a similar game for next year. Contact Kili if you want to play!

Thanks go out to all those ex-provincial players who participated in the game but did not tackle anybody. The chemist reported an undue product-run on anything that might help bruises and flatulance.

"Where the hell is Tarkastad?"

"Look in your atlas, you dope. It's halfway between heaven and the Karoo!"

TROEPIE TROUBLE

MAN, IF EVER YOU wanted to see a bugger-up you should have been at Rooikop base just outside of Walvis Bay during those days. A hell of a lot of army okes who had defaulted badly were sent there as a sort of punishment, you know. They were the most slapgat troepies you could ever see, ou swaer! The truth of the matter was that nobody, but nobody, could tell those bliksems what to do. They like ruled the place, you see.

First of all, they did not want to fight on the Border. Second of all, they did not like people with rank, like corporals, sergeants, lieutenants and captains and so on. According to army regulations, paragraph something or other, these okes had to have one hour per day with exercises outside, you follow. These blokes were so far gone that D.B. and short-rations meant nothing to them. You remember that film, 'The Dirty Dozen', where some Yankee jailbirds stuffed up the whole of the German Army by themselves. Well, if they let these okes loose on them they would have moered the Russians as well... before breakfast, I tell you.

From eleven to twelve o'clock every day so to speak was the buitekant parade and everybody had to get outside and walk around while the corporals checked out the barracks for any hidden things like knives, cigarettes, dirty books, porno and AK-47s. Nee ek maak maar grappies! About the AKs, I mean! One day they found a hymn book hollowed out with boom inside. Another time they found a matchbox with a frenchie inside. Ja, today they call it a condom.

To give you some idea how slap these troeps were ... one of their tricks was to carry a pal out onto the parade ground and put him down on his back in the sun where he like thought he was a Hollywood star, taking off his dark glasses and breathing onto them, then rubbing them on his sleeve. He used to pull his hat over his eyes and wave to everybody. He was in for manslaughter because he killed another troep during a fight by hitting him over the head with a bottle. Nee, oh, hell, ou maat, these okes were first league, I tell you.

Another bloke was walking around picking up every small stone and looking underneath it and holding it up to the sun. He would then sit down and let the sand run through his fingers as if he was looking for diamonds. He would then take off his boots and tip them to get rid of any sand and look deeply into them. Another time he would put his ear to the ground with his arse in the air as if he was a blêrrie Bushman tracker. I tell you! He told the corporal that he was listening for the truck to take him to the hotel and that under the small stones he might find his discharge papers from the general.

Nee, o gats, I can tell you much more about those boytjies. But you asked me about rugby, not so? Okay. Some major decided that they should play a rugby game against each other. The plan was that A Block would choose a team, as well as B Block and so on. It went down to E Block you see. The trouble started when some bright troep said that there was five teams so how could a semi-final be played or something like that. After lights-out the arguments went on and on and the C.O. threatened to turn the water hoses onto them if they did not shut up and go to sleep.

The major issued an order that the chosen delegates from the Blocks should meet him for discussions about the game in his office. The whole bloody compound pitched up because of democracy. The meeting was put off for a future date. Two weeks later the chosen spokesman for that lot said that he had the answer to the problem. It had been decided that E Block would not play because they were the kindertjies and had only recently arrived in detention. Problem solved. Okay! Lekka!

So now there had to be a semi-final between A, B, C and D Blocks. Okay, permission granted, no problem! It was decided to use ping-pong balls with the letters on them put on with black ink. They put them in a bag and the corporal had to close his eyes and draw out the balls. This all took place after supper in the dining room. It was all fluit-fluit and the rattling of spoons on plates as the draw was settled. A plays C, and B plays D. Everybody trooped out all satisfied like, to make their plans for the coming games. The major ordered that the games would be played the coming Saturday. A versus C at one o'clock, and B versus D at three o' clock.

During the week there were queries as to who would be the referees. The major put his foot down and told them that he would appoint fair refs who had experience and if there was any more buggering around eveything would be cancelled. They asked if they could have oranges at half-time. Okay, no problem, as long as they behaved themselves on the field and played according to the rules. One team manager asked for a set of rules and was booted out of the major's office.

The major was not taking any more crap from anybody and ordered sixty T-shirts from the army depot in Windhoek. Thirty khaki ones and thirty white ones. You could play kaalpoot or with takkies but use your own socks if you wanted to. Fixed up! No problem! The major declared an open day for the base so as to have spectators from Walvis Bay where Number Two Battalion was based. He also invited the navy and as an afterthought also the divers. The medics were put on full duty for the game as well as a section of the Riot Squad made up of MPs, you understand. The Military Police would man the hoses if something went wrong.

I do not want to bore you, Graham, with the details of the games that Saturday afternoon but it went down very well, as they say. From the kick-off it was total warfare in the dust of the base. Sometimes the ref could not blow his whistle because it was full of dust and this made some players gatvol. Everybody seemed to be offside and there were a lot of late tackles and torn T-shirts. One player had his pants pulled down and he had nothing on underneath. He then pulled down another bloke's pants and got a red card. He went off to cheers from everybody. Six blokes were admitted to the hospital. Both games were over and everybody was invited to the final next Saturday.

Man, now something strange happened at Rooikop during the week. It happened just before the final game on that Saturday. I will tell you as I go along. The kommandant for the region decided that he wanted to see for himself how things were going and came over from Windhoek, but wanted a parade and march-past before the game. In the past this outfit of tronk birds and Swapo prisoners were a disaster on parade. They could not care a fok for anything, you understand. Anyway, this young corporal from the Eastern Cape, who was kicked out of Infantary School for being too good at sport, seemed to have got through to them.

I was there that day, ou Graham, and I could not believe my own eyes! There was no band and the men formed up quietly outside the main gate in three platoons. The young corporal was the only oke shouting commands at the head of the columns. "Peletonne! Aandag!" When their feet hit the ground it sounded like one big stomp! And they all shouted "uumph!" It was blêrrie scary.

"In column of threes, from the right, quick maaarch!" They moved like one man, I promise you! "Links, regs, links, regs!" and here they came towards the major's platform for the salute.

The corporal yelled, "Peleton A, ogies regs!" Like one man I tell you again, but they did not salute. The other sections went through the same drill and it was blêrrie perfect. I don't think the major could believe what was going on in front of his own eyes. The spectators clapped, as the next order was, "Eyes front!" They halted farther on and were smartly dismissed.

They chanted, "Een, twee, drie. Een, twee, drie, een!" They fell out all slapgat again and went to change for the game.

The ref blew his whistle and the spectators wanted

to know when the hell this game was going to start. Eventually the players trooped onto the field and kind of took up their positions. The kick-off was slap and the players like walked around the ball slowly like nobody wanted to pick it up. Somebody then did and like waltzed a walk with his elbows in the wind looking from right to left, to see who would tackle him. The major was blowing up slowly on his seat while the spectators were starting to laugh and enjoy themselves. It was the slowest game you have ever seen in your life, and the players looked all serious with dented brows from concentration.

The ref got the hell in and walked off tapping his head with his finger while shaking his head from side to side. All the players now stopped and shrugged their shoulders with hands on hips, shaking their heads from side to side. I looked at the major on the raised platform and could see murder in his eyes. The spectators cheered and laughed again because they all thought that it was supposed to be like this, you understand. The major looked around and saw that the crowd was enjoying themselves so he like smiled and nodded his head for all to see.

The Eastern Cape corporal strode onto the field and blew his whistle and ordered a set scrum in the middle of the field. The response was immediate and we saw a game of rugby like you cannot believe. The okes from the Boland and Western Province areas climbed in and produced rugby uit die boonste rakke as the spreekwoord says. The tackling was first-time and the dust danced around them but they did not care. A game is mos a game, ou swaer, as they say. I cannot remember who won the game because of the changes and swopping sides among the players. When the final whistle blew they gave three cheers with a clenched fist, which was on the banned list, as you know!

Now the army was in a bit of a spot here, you see. They had really done nothing wrong, so to speak, except give the black-power salute, which was banned. How could they punish all the players except for extra duties and all that? They were all doing that already in one way or another. They could not reduce their food rations because that was against I think the Geneva Convention or something like that. I do not know what happened at the Staff meeting on the following Monday but on the notice board was pinned:

Recreation facilities will return to normal procedures according to the Defence Act and under no circumstances will team sports be allowed without special permission from the Camp Kommandant.

This was on paper behind a sliding-glass plate and locked in the corridor outside of the Staff office. A couple of days later the order had been turned around and pinned back onto the board behind the glass. It simply said:

Dankie, my Basie, vir die fokken lekka jol!

It was signed 'Gatiepie'. Can you believe it!

THE COMMUNISTS ARE COMING

THE RAILWAY JUNCTION OF Alicedale near Grahamstown usually slumbered its way through the hot summers, with noises like railway engines letting off steam and the clanking of trucks being shunted. Shouts like, "kom, kom, stadig, ja, okay nog tien tree, goed so, okay fine!" were commonplace as the shunters coupled the trucks with the slamming sounds of metal on metal. A shrill whistle and the unmistakable sound of empty milk cans being loaded onto open trucks for return to the farms along the milk route.

The coaling depot was farther down the line, as well as the large water tank with its elephant-like trunk dangling down, waiting for some thirsty S.A.R. & H. railway engine to start slurping water for its boilers. The local hotel with its rather small bar took care of the slurping of the drivers, stokers, signalmen, tappies, shunters and everybody else involved in keeping a railway junction alive. This was the Railway Hotel. The stationmaster, with his Hitler-like moustache and smart, black uniform, never went there because his wife said it was an evil place to go on your own. For relaxation he drank in the toolshed next to his pigeon hok. When he started cooing and talking to his birds his wife called him in for supper.

The monotomy of this junction was occasionally broken by the inspector of railways from Port Elizabeth paying a visit and inviting the stationmaster and his wife for dinner, as well as the chief foreman of works and his wife, the chief storeman and his wife, as well as the mother-in-law, but Stoorie had to pay for her. The venue was the Railway Hotel. Hymie used to excel himself with roasts and good wine and often served his exalted guests himself. Rebecca stayed out of sight and ran the kitchen with an iron fist. She never smiled and often Hymie rolled his eyes towards the heavens after instructions flew at him from all sides. He was happy because his only son was at Rhodes University, not so far away, studying for his B.A.. One day he could take over the hotel and Hymie would go down to P.E. and lie on the beach for the rest of his life. Without Rebecca!

Rebecca was constantly talking to Hymie about the I.O.U. book, which he had opened for the railway blokes to drink on tick. He calmed her down and reminded her that winter was coming soon and that rugby matches would be played on the Railway Rec and that all debts would be paid by betting on the railway side. The main game was always against the Rhodes University third side, which had never won in Alicedale in ten years. They were not allowed to. In good fun the students betted against themselves and so the whole problem was sorted out. The students had a rave. They put money into the pockets of the railway blokes who in turn paid off their debts at the Railway Hotel.

The stationmaster was always uneasy about this flagrant violation of the law as gambling was not allowed on government property, and that included the rugby field. It was built for them by the government and maintained by funds from the subs that the players were supposed to pay at the beginning of each season. Weeding and cutting the grass was either done by labourers from the two sheds or by prisoners who needed a day's outing in the sunshine

The prison guard always had the traditional assegaai with him as a status symbol though he never had to use it.

"Hey, Stampvas! Have you heard about our fixtures for the season?" asked Kallie as he offered his fellow stoker a Gold Dollar cigarette.

"Nee nog nie. I'm waiting for the meeting on Friday night, then Bakkies will tell us."

Kallie smiled like a man with a secret that he could not keep to himself. "Well, Bakkies got back last night from the E.P. Rugby Union meeting in P.E. and he told me who our first match was against!"

Stampvas was alert and muttered, "Toe tell me, man. Just don't say it is against General Motors because they are looking for us after that last game when we got a penalty in the last minute under their posts."

Kallie took a long draw on his cigarette and watched the smoke go straight up like a burnt offering, which has been accepted. "Ag, no man, it's easier than that, we are playing the communists from Grahamstown."

"Bliksem, what luck! We'll have two points on the log from our first game. Those long-haired Molotovs are not allowed to win here!"

Kallie finished off by stating his feelings. "Look man, never trust a communist from a university. Remember what our M.P. told us before the last election in that same hall over there."

Stampvas knitted his brow and uttered solemnly, "Ja, you are right. Ons sal hulle moet watch."

They both ambled over to the Railway Hotel for a game of darts.

"Ons sal niks praat nie, but we know, okay." Kallie kicked at a stone and concluded, "Ons is okay, okay?"

"Ja dis okay met my, okay?"

Agreement was reached and the secret was safe.

At the meeting the fixtures were revealed and copies distributed to all the players of the Alicedale Rugby Club, as well as an appeal for subs in order to be able to pay Hymie for snacks after the games for the season etc., etc., etc.! The railway blokes were armed with valuable information, which they could check with their work schedules.

Somebody lamented from the corner, "Dis kak vir my. I will be in blêrrie Kookhuis to meet the P.E.–De Aar train on that day!"

It now became like the Johannesburg Stock Exchange with deals being done all over the place. Who could play and when? The sound went up a notch, but this always happened on this night at the start of the season.

Four rather clapped-out student cars arrived from Grahamstown on that Saturday and skidded to a halt outside the Railway Hotel.

"What came out of the cars was like a group of blêrrie tourists visiting the River in France. Ja, no, what do you call it? Ja, jy's reg … the French Riviera, you say. Ja, that is it ou Graham!"

Little Hekkies was on his bicycle and peddled flat

out for home. "Ma, Pa! Hulle is hier, die een oom het draad in sy oor en die ander een het wit sakdoeke om sy kop gedraai!" Message delivered. He chased around Alicedale on his Phillips 22-inch bike shouting, "Hulle is hier, hulle is hier!" His poenskop was bobbing up and down in the sun and his young eyes was blazing with excitement as he skidded around the dusty streets of the junction. "Baie van die ooms dra donker brille en een het twee kanne bier in sy hand!"

Into the lounge trooped all the Rhodes players led by their captain, Doc. Hymie met them with a diplomatic smile and escorted them to a room close to the showers down the long passage. He stopped, his mouth open in surprise. His son Solomon, called Solly, was with them.

"Hi, Dad, meet my captain, Doc, and all my teammates."

Hymie held out his hand, "Pleezed to meet you Doctor. So pleezed to have you with us. Our doctor from Cookhouse is on leave and is fishing on the Wild Coast. We now feel safe." Solly beamed and led the Thirsty Thirds down the passage with a swagger.

Klein Hekkies shouted to his dad, who was just coming out of his front gate, "Pa, Pa, weet wat? Solly speel vir die kommuniste!"

Stampvas stopped in his tracks. This was now a serious thing. His mind whirled, as he was captain for this match and owed Hymie quite a lot of money for drinks over the last month, and so did all his teammates. What would happen if Solly knew nothing about the set-up of paying off debts? Hymie always told his son that a winner is a winner in life. He was always

189

told by his grandmother that a "boer maak 'n plan!" He dashed over and slipped through the back door into the kitchen where Rebecca was busy cleaning up.

Doc led his side onto the field and decided that Solly would play flyhalf, because Rhodes were not allowed to win. This was traditional. Solly wanted to prove to his parents that he was now one of the manne. Hymie arrived at the game and cheered his boytjie on. He had never before been down to the field and he was walking up and down the touchline giving advice to the communists.

"Goeie Vader, ek vertel vir jou dat die klein Joodse losskakel soos 'n Springbok gespeel het. Voor die Alicedale manne hulle ogies kon uitvee was hulle 8-0 agter. Solly slaag met twee drieë en die vervyfskop. Hy was besig om die blêrrie game te oorheers!"

The Rhodes captain, Doc was getting frantic. They had to lose this game! It was traditional. If they won, no free beers for the students and maybe tyres let down and all that kak. He told the scrumhalf to give Solly 'shit ball'. But Solly picked up any pass that was thrown at him. Half-time and a team talk next to the fence while sucking on the oranges from Kirkwood. Doc told Solly to play fullback to learn more about defence. The boy's eyes lit up when Doc told him that all great Springboks had to go through this learning curve.

Early in the second half Railway got two penalties for offsides from Doc at flyhalf. It was now Rhodes 8, Alicedale 6. The 4.30 goods-and-milk train steamed into the station and Flippie pulled the whistle three times as he looked across at the battle before his eyes.

Oh, Graham, he told me, stuff the coaling siding and the water pipe, he was going to run across the tracks and see the game! His stoker and guardsman from the back of the train did the same. The stationmaster had another Klippies and Coke and watched from his big window. His wife was still knitting rompers for the grandchildren and listening to the radio programme, 'Liefde in ons Lewe' as well as 'The House of Mary Laine'.

Things were becoming very critical out there. The communists had to lose! Doc was at his wits' end. Five minutes to go. He told his men to back off. Railway were out on their feet and did not know what to do. A heavenly angel appeared in the form of Rebecca lamenting the Sabbath and that Solly should be with her in her hour of need. Like a good Yiddisha boy he left the field and went arm in arm up to the hotel. No fullback, so Kallie put up an up-and-under. The Rhodes okes stood back and the bounce saw Vaalseun over in the corner. The conversion was missed and the final whistle blew. Alicedale 9, Rhodes 8. Blêrrie close, hey!

Ek will jou vertel dat daardie aand in Alicedale iets besonders was. Everybody was happy and the gramaphone was turned on and the dancing started. 'Rock Around the Clock', 'Jailhouse Rock', 'Teacher's Pet' and al daardie kak! The Rhodes okes were given free rooms for the night. The local police sergeant told them to close at eleven o'clock. They all agreed and the bar stayed open until midnight. Rebecca was all pronk, pronk and served a free breakfast to her Solly's friends the next morning.

The railwaymaster had now finished his bottle of

Klippies and his wife was injured on duty by stabbing herself in the finger with a knitting needle. The youngsters had great fun playing in the sand outside the hotel and watching the rugby players come out, unzipping their pants and looking at the stars.

"Pa, what is a communist?"

Kallie smiled and answered, "I am not certain. Go ask your mother."

FAMOUS PROVINCIAL UNIONS AND OLDER CLUBS

Western Province

Founded:	1883
Colours:	royal blue and white
Headquarters:	Newlands, Cape Town

Clubs:

Gardens	1879
Hamiltons	1875
Paarl	1883
Stellenbosch	1880
U.C.T.	1882
Villagers	1875

Griqualand West

Founded:	1886
Colours:	peacock blue and white
Headquarters:	De Beers Stadium, Kimberley

Clubs:

Boshof	1894
De Beers	1893
Pirates	1884

Eastern Province

Founded:	1888
Colours:	black and red
Headquarters:	Boet Erasmus Stadium

Clubs:

Grahamstown	1893

Crusaders	1887
Humansdorp	1888
Olympics	1881
Swifts	1890

Transvaal

Founded:	1889
Colours:	red and white
Headquarters:	Ellis Park, Johannesburg

Clubs:

Diggers	1894
Pirates	1888
Roodepoort	1899
Wanderers	1888

Natal

Founded:	1890
Colours:	black and white
Headquarters:	King's Park, Durban

Clubs:

| Berea Rovers | 1898 |
| Old Collegians | 1888 |

**Border
(originally Frontier)**

Founded:	1891
Colours:	chocolate brown and white
Headquarters:	Border Rugby Union Ground, later Basil Kenyon Stadium, East London

Clubs:

| Alberts | 1878 |

Buffaloes	1877
Cathcart	1888
Elliott	1895
Pirates	1887
Swifts	1882

Orange Free State

Founded:	1895
Colours:	orange and white
Headquarters:	Springbok Park, (Free State Stadium, Bloemfontein)

Clubs:

University	1912

South Western Districts

Founded:	1899
Colours:	green and white
Headquarters:	George Stadium, George

Clubs:

Beaufort West	1885
George	1882
Mossel Bay	1882
Oudtshoorn	1883
Riversdale	1890
Swellendam	1883

North Eastern Cape
(originally North Eastern Districts)

Founded:	1903
Colours:	old gold and black

Headquarters:	Cradock Rugby Ground, Cradock

Clubs:

Burgersdorp	1887
Colesburg	1892
Cradock Rovers	1882

South West Africa (originally Damaraland)

Founded:	1916
Colours:	sky blue and dark red
Headquarters:	South Western Stadium, Windhoek

Clubs:

Harlequins	1917
Windhoek	1917
United	1916

Western Transvaal

Founded:	1920
Colours:	green and red
Headquarters:	Olen Park, Potchefstroom

Clubs:

Klerksdorp	1890
Potchefstroom Town	1885

Northern Transvaal

Founded:	1938
Colours:	light blue and dark blue
Headquarters:	Loftus Versfeld, Pretoria

Clubs:

Pretoria	1888

Boland

Founded:	1939
Colours:	black and old gold
Headquarters:	Boland Stadium, Wellington

Clubs:

Caledon	1884
Malmsbury	1881
Montagu	1882
Morreesburg	1898
Porterville	1899
Robertson	1885
Tulbach	1886
Wellington Paarl	1882
Worcester	1883

North Western Cape

Founded:	1967
Colours:	royal blue and orange
Headquarters:	Danie Kluis Stadium, Upington

Clubs:

Kakamas	1899
Keimos	1899
Kenhardt	1899
Upington	1908

Eastern Transvaal

Founded:	1947
Colours:	red/white (originally maroon)
Headquarters:	Pam Brink Stadium, Springs

Clubs:

Boksburg E.R.P.M.	1894

Heidelberg   1899

Far North
Founded: 1968
Colours: royal blue and red
Headquarters: Pietersburg Stadium,
                          Pietersburg

Clubs:
Pietersburg   1902

Northern Free State
Founded: 1968
Colours: purple and gold
Headquarters: North Western Stadium,
                          Welkom

Clubs:
Kroonstad Wanderers   1917

Eastern Free State
Founded: 1968
Colours: white and dark blue
Headquarters: Goble Park, Bethlehem
Clubs:
Ficksburg   1895

South Eastern Transvaal
Founded: 1968
Colours: dove grey and red
Headquarters: Johan van Riebeeck Stadium,
                          Witbank

Clubs:
Ermelo   1891

| Middelburg | 1896 |
| Standerton | 1888 |

Stellaland

Founded:	1975
Colours:	fawn, red and white
Headquarters:	Rugby Grounds, Vryburg

Clubs:

| Mafeking | 1903 |

Northern Natal

Founded:	1973
Colours:	green and gold
Headquarters:	Arbor Park, Newcastle

Clubs:

| Newcastle | 1890 |
| Volksrust | 1898 |

Vaal Triangle

Founded:	1984
Colours:	turquoise and orange
Headquarters:	D.P. de Villiers Stadium, Sasolburg

Clubs:

| Heilbron | 1899 |
| Koppies | 1899 |

Lowveld

Founded:	1985
Colours:	gold and emerald green
Headquarters:	Rugby Grounds, Nelspruit

Clubs:

| Barberton | 1904 |

As the reader can imagine there may well be other older clubs that were established on the platteland before the Anglo-Boer War of 1899–1902. Records are difficult to come by and many may well have been destroyed during the conflict.